EYES

of a

CHAMPION

JONATHAN HARDY

EYES OF A CHAMPION

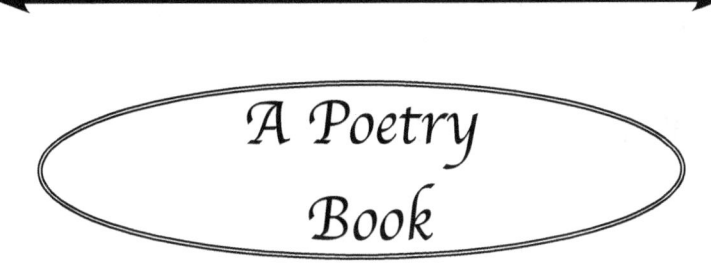

A Poetry Book

DZ
NC
SMITH

Books may be purchased by contacting the publisher and author at designzbyncsmith@yahoo.com; 248-763-0878:

Cover Design: Designz by N.C. Smith, LLC
Interior Design: Designz by N.C. Smith, LLC
Publisher: Designz by N.C. Smith, LLC
Editor: Jonathan Hardy
ISBN: 978-0-9895850-0-2
ISBN: 978-0-9895850-1-9(e-book)
1. Poetry 2. Inspirational
First Edition
Printed in United States of America

First Printing , 2014

Dedication page.....

Firstly, I dedicate this book to my Lord and Savior, Jesus Christ, for saving me, making the ultimate sacrifice for you, and setting the ultimate example for all. Without him I'm nothing, but with him nothing is impossible...

Secondly, I dedicate this to my family, for your everlasting support, for your encouragement, and for your love. I have no idea where I would be without any of you, and I am grateful to have you all in my life..

Lastly, I dedicate this to you, the audience in which I speak. Those striving for, and looking to maintain, greatness so their world might become limitless; I hope that I am merely a Good Samaritan on the road to your dreams....

Much Love,

Table of Contents

TABLE OF CONTENTS

H

A Message from the Author

To the ones who have already had the chance to read my thoughts and to those curious enough to embark on the journey through my poetry, I sincerely thank you. I thank you because you are the courageous ones looking for change, for something different, overall seeking positivity. As you may have noticed, the world hasn't really developed a very constructive image of minorities, and a lot of times, honestly, we haven't helped them. With our ill-mannered behaviors, unruly actions, reckless practices, and negative attitudes it is not hard to understand why we are consistently stereotyped. Now please don't misunderstand me, these things are not always synonymous with strictly minorities in general, but more often than not, this is the representation we are shown.

Many of us, being young people of these New Generations, were brought up in terrible surroundings. Areas that are known to breed negative thoughts, words, and actions that lead to damaging results. With this burden that we carry on our back, usually unloaded from our environment, we fall subject to become what we have seen on a regular basis. As those-looking to make a quick dollar and side-step our way to riches, turning to drugs and alcohol from peer pressured influence or to blot our stressful reality, avoiding education, and the list continues. Knowing this, I was inspired to begin writing poetry because there are many things in our day to day lives that make us often times struggle and even worse, give up. If there is no one that is there backing or encouraging us to better ourselves and move forward, we can easily get sidetracked. This is why I wanted to write a book that would push everyone, of all races and ages, to do and be better (but since "we" are the future, a lot of my works are aimed at the youth).

If you are anything like I was, you most likely weren't rushing to read another book, and I can't blame you. Reading was not my favorite pastime but when I realized that I wanted to do better and BE better I found that this was the primary way to advance. That being said, I wanted to supply the masses with something that would facilitate reading without the regimen of drudgery that may have been the norm. To supply positivity in a different way, through poetry with different rhyme-schemes, and where the readers are able to see themselves in the things they read; so I guarantee that this will be different. These poems were written to connect with you on a personal level, and give you a constructive image of the future. They not only address what is but more-so, what could be. Since this is the case, I do want my readers to keep in mind that these journeys contain a large measure of realism. My works depict people in evolutionary states, so they may include words and ideals that can be viewed as offensive. This is not the intention-to offend or maliciously hurt anyone, but rather give the reader a representation of how someone can transition. How they can have a pivotal moment causing the subject to move from realism to optimism, no matter how bumpy the road may be in between. So if you are one that will judge my work, I ask that you do it in a "holistic" state.

If you take the time to read this book, you have my sincerest gratitude. Whoever you may be, I want you to know that I believe in you, I appreciate you and I'm proud that you have even considered reading my work. This poetry describes many individuals, including myself, and other that I've seen through my own eyes, and it's funny how closely we as people relate. I've seen the degradation of violence and the effects of drugs first hand, along with many different stories I've heard, and I find they never end as a pretty picture. If you are contemplating going down this road, feeling lost or that you have something to prove, let me tell you now, you don't have to go this route. I believe there is a greater purpose for your life and it all starts when you live with a positive perspective. I would love to tell you that a constructive change will make you popular and make everyone love you but it often times sets you apart. In the end though, the things that you gain are irreplaceable. The ability to look at any situation optimistically, to believe in yourself, to love yourself and others, to forgive AND forget, and to largely enjoy peace-knowing that everything will eventually be alright. These things will come to you when you decide that you want to be different, be better, and be great. I hope that you will make that choice, and if my poems motivate you to do so, then I am thankful that a source much greater than myself was able to transform you. These are my thoughts, opinions, and views on subjects that I feel need to be addressed and I hope that you are able to enjoy but also able take something with you from each poem.

Lastly, I only ask of you one thing, and that is…as you ascend, that you reach back and bring others with you; share what you now know. I expect great things from each and every one of you, and may you forever prosper…

Yours Truly,

EYES

of a

CHAMPION

Eyes of a Champion

(In honor of the Olympics)

Passion-filled purpose; trapped,
In two focusing pupils.
Concentrating through goal-driven eyes,
Rarely recalling the feeling of neutral.

The windows of a reliant soul,
Feeding on the image of competition.
Aspirer of a unique task,
Conqueror of an alleged impossible mission.

With excellent precision combined with endurance,
Sight set entirely on the finishing outcome.
Emotional face, but unwavering eyes,
Unsympathetic to size-the call of greatness beckons.

And the singular answer appears only to one,
One-that courageously stands the test of time.
Confidently pursuing an incomplete paved road,
Stretching further to extend the line.

There to leave a name signed,
Which brown, amber, and blue-printed eyes envision.
Settled in a golden heart-then revitalized,
To externally wear gold of a champion….

Fear

There's something hiding in my system,
That likes to arise when I make a critical decision,
It never aids-in fact it delays me,
Encages me in a solitary prison.

It hibernates inside me,
As bears in a cave,
And like the same-when it's my springtime,
It slowly arises again.

Supplying pessimistic thoughts-
That will try and hold me back,
To break up my solid ground-
So I can't keep my foundation intact.

The earthquake that shakes up my track,
So that I can't run the course,
The disconnecter that removes my plug,
From a motivational source.

Water that puts out the torch-
That guides me toward my goal,
The terrible hand it deals me,
So that I will choose to fold.

Its presence alone won't let me progress,
Wanting me to end up a carcass-
That was taken out, as,
it's successfully hit target.

Employed, taking my "drive"-
Only to "park it",
Valet serviced,-putting me in,
a garage section that's the darkest.

It places a mirage-
In front of my view,
Showing me that I can't do,
Some of the things that I aspire to.

The tree that only harvests spoiled fruit,
So I'll drink of its fermented juice,
Causing me to sit-dizzily,
With my senses obtuse.

Consistently placing a mind set failure
In the depths of my structure,
So my movement is in reverse,
Ever since I let FEAR rupture.

...My mind,
An emotion unrecognized ***by*** my heart,
My soul waiting for full course meals,
But fear causes me to order a la carte.

Picking and choosing small objectives,
When I can handle as large as they come,
But the risk of failing-
Causes me instead to run from.

So I live a fear-stricken life,
Frozen like deer in oncoming vehicle's headlights,
Since my mind won't go against it-scared,
Unready to fight.

Unprepared for whatever justification,
Or not confident enough to advance without verification,
So like a felon on probation,
Fear is the judge that limits me.

With this internal civil war,
My mind never lets my heart be free,
My inner-me, the eminent enemy-In this life's further pursuit,
With this weight attached firmly to my shoes,
I'll never reach my highest altitude...

EQUALITY

Black and White, with pedals below,
Strings behind, attached to the same frame,
Side-by-side, set on the same row,
Various amounts and levels, yet in the same plane,

With unpressed pedals, keys are played staccato,
Each note hits like a drop – of rain,
But notes held together, paint pictures like Picasso,
With an extra step taken, their effects sustain,

Piano keys that sit peaceful, ignorant of their color,
Until pushed to work together, the key of their destiny,
To make chords, that have harmonious melodies like no other,
Symphonious flavored creations ad-libbed with out recipes,

White and Black, yet still the same are sisters and brothers,
Not focusing on color, and are immensely useful indeed,
Because this painted color, just sits as their cover,
With the same internal strings which gives them equality…

An Intangible Commodity

I see our elders as…
Early Leaders Dedicated Earnestly Raising Society,
With wisdom, knowledge, and experience,
A rare intangible commodity.

Reminding me of antique pottery,
Holding the dirty soil of this filthy world,
Adding minerals, nutrients, and lucid...
Refreshing water droplets, impearled.

Most were hurled from the ancestry of slaves,
Working on farms and plantations,
And I believe some seniors still plant to this day,
Not from tradition, but rather, them coming
from a nurturing generation.

They hold the ability to mold God's creation,
Into the rightful-upstanding handiwork we should be,
Using lessons from their past situations,
Spreading the good from their history.

And transparently sharing the bad stories as well,
Knowing there is importance in telling the whole truth,
For some, this comes easy, for most this is hard,
And for others they're reluctant, like a child
pulling a loose tooth.

The youth, even if it sounds in some way illogical,
In every way-shape-and-form, need to hear that,
Because prying into our lives, without revealing
a holistic view of your past,
Is constantly adding space to this generational gap.

We've been known to act, at our age,
As if we need no help, knowing it all,
Quite the contrary, we just hate the act of perfection,
Coming from teachers pretending that they never fall.

We really don't mind tales,
As long as "tall" isn't the format they all come in,
Pleasant conditions are great, but it touches us knowing…
Our seniors made it through hell and high waters, with a grin.

With the society we live in,
Old age turns into something hard to come by,
Either because we chose not to adhere to direction,
Or broken families passed down no advice.

I hear we live twice as a child,
But only once as an adult,
And it seems that what is taught the first time around,
Hits us in the second youth, in a way that's more heartfelt.

That's why true elders have warmth that melts,
Some strongholds with forgiveness and love,
As they get closer to meeting their creator,
Being more like the lord, is all they dream of.

Though sometimes, it seems tough,
They criticize only to construct, sincerely,
Even if it comes in a formation that's ancient,
Like the words following after "Hear ye, Hear ye."

Either way, they've had a hand on the rudder that steers me,
Because I've learned to truly listen,
Enlightening me, when I thought I was complete,
Revealing certain things that I still had missing.

They tend to be the good Samaritans,
Helping to repave our lives potholes,
Because elders don't just walk the path to old age,
They successfully consecrate that long road.

They, like a treasure chest of gold,
Have priceless valuables inside,
The backbone of every culture,
Teaching us in what we should take pride.

Supplying the determination to strive past all failures,
For victory is just past our fears,
And when that day comes, to be modest,
Not labeling ourselves by accomplishments and careers.

Nor are we defined by our peers,
But instead by the qualities we contain,
Because when we are judged, there is never an "us,"
But only one person that will be named.

And these, are just a few things that came,
From the mouths of our seasoned vets,
And just a few more reasons why…
They deserve our utmost respect.

For the Lord lets us wake to experience the present,
And our seniors allow us to glimpse into the past,
But only when we use both effectively,
Will we, too, create a legacy for the future, that will last…

I CHOOSE

In a different arena now, where I'm from was just books,
It was illustrated to be this way, but reality presents a new look.
So shook... by the looks, that I constantly receive,
Because what I represent, most aint tryna see.
Excuse me? I'd rather you talk to me like a man-
Not a child, I'm not ignorant-people, I do understand.
Don't hold my hand, just give me a chance to stand
so I can plant my feet,
But solidity, they not giving me, so I can easily accept defeat.
Feels like I'm being tricked into thoughts to better myself,
Was taught knowledge before wealth,
both "they" hold in hands on the highest shelf.
So we can dig in our pockets and see how
much we're willing to pay...
And sorry niggaz, on this product, there ain't no lay-away,
Thought school would do me better, instead taught me it wasn't needed.
They teach us-rape us for money, the real world tells us to delete it,
So how can I succeed when my accounts;
the student loans bleed?
Got knowledge you don't want or need, not strong
enough to climb that tree,
Looking up at people not willing to help, and no
one behind to push me.
Still technically not free, just wanting to breathe,
So I can get my hands on some cheese, without the 3rd degree.
And it's sad that we can't be glad, with the position that we have,
Where people got your back, using knowledge you
have and adding to that,
And at the end of the day-happy to be improving your stack.
But with this lack of motivation-I'll choose to grab the click-clack,
And yup, not looking back the side hustle begins.
The door is wide open and my foot is itchin' to slide in,
........so ready..........so ready..........
But something keeps stopping me,
I'm steadily tryna force it, but my limbs lack grease.
As I'm unveil an epiphany; that getting wealth from the streets
and living to tell it,
Is a fool's fantasy that barely happens, even when
you've been hood developed.
But I'll embellish at the fact that I am the underdog,
So I can turn on these low lights to escape all this fog.
Work hard to reach my potential no matter how much bull is still sent,
And be that breath of fresh air out this stankin' environment.
Because I'll make it, even if the corporate offices are so egotistic,
And be proud at the fact that I wasn't just another statistic...

If We'd Only Look Around

From the ground ascending to clouds,
Natural beauty beheld,
If only we'd ever look around,
Stepping outside of ourselves.

Fast-paced lives cause us to ignore,
What our creator made beside us,
Available at anytime to explore,
But our lack of interest denies thrust.

Why be fascinated with earth's mysteries?
Seen them everyday of our lives,
But only take notice to our being,
Attention elsewhere is wasted time.

Stems connected to golden pedals,
Swans presence on still ponds,
Leaves in fall turn golden metal,
Acres of vegetable grown lawns.

Waves rolling of various depths,
Hills rolling beside mountainside,
Insects closest to our grave of death,
Birds elevated highest in skies.

By all this we daily walk,
Blind to just see city influence,
Those that have interest; we mock,
Though we all should share their same pursuance.

To sit still with no sound,
Natural beauty to behold,
If only we look around,
We may see more inside our soul…

Disconnecting Strings

When I met you, we clicked,
Not like that of puzzle pieces,
But yet you still moved me,
Like the study of telekinesis.
Our thesis subject was "friends,"
And we complimented each other,
We kept it real on the daily,
As more secrets became uncovered.
Never smothered, but evenly spaced,
When needing a push, we gave a nudge,
Lent an ear when it was needed,
And what was voiced, we left un-judged.
But like a smudge, we lost clarity,
Seeing each other in a different light,
Sides of the scale became uneven,
Noticing one's feelings intensified.
No high-rise, was in your front row,
Being up-front with you from the jump,
Wasn't really looking at you in that way,
So how we got twisted, has me stumped.
This speed-bump formed in our road,
From the many moments that we've shared,
The laughs, smiles, hugs, and long conversations,
Til' for me, in a different way, you cared.
Which has me scared to reveal honestly,
Because I would hate to see you in pain,
But reality is, when I voice my truth,
Our connection will drastically change.
Never the same will we interact,
Without my heartfelt reciprocation,
So these strings do not connect,
Bringing your eyes rain-like precipitation.
So our relation is no longer harmless,
While we both now walk on egg-shells,
With this subtle awkwardness between us,
Makes our attempts to casually carry-on, fail.

And your frail vulnerability shows why,
Sensitive to the new situation,
Caught off-guard by the way I reacted,
Adjusting, like foreign habitat adaptation.
A transformation leaving you confused,
Being rejected by someone so close,
Someone that almost knows you best,
Often times tends to hurt you the most.
Leaving you froze with the question, why?
Why not me? Why not us?
Sometimes the symbol between two people,
Is much further than the sign plus,
If you know too much, or not enough,
Or not wanting to change what ya'll have.
Trying to keep this entity subliminal,
Still, inevitably, it changed, imagine that,
Or they don't attract to you in that manner,
Because they relate you as kin.
Whatever the case may happen to be,
I'll choose not to weigh-in,
On this table-end with your cards laid out,
And my I.O.U. of "Why?" on top.
Makes me fold with no questions asked,
Freely giving up this type of pot,
My reasoning thought, only makes things worse,
It never helps to swallow this pill.
So as I reject, I also protect,
From inflicting your soul further ill,
This I feel, is hardest to translate,
Despite which language you choose.
That no matter how much more you liked me,
I can only be a friend to you…

I Don't Know

This is me, or is it? I believe I'm so official with it,
But at the same time, I find, my inside feels a little different,
I'm afraid to present it and be identified as unauthentic,
Because I rather not choose to throw myself to the critics,
And hear them chirp like crickets, so I leave my windows tinted,
You'll never see me down and out; to you I'll always be winning,

From the beginning, I was taught to present it this way,
May not be the best representation, but with me, it's ok,
Choose to stay with the tinted glass, to show you a reflection of yourself,
So while I'm with you we resemble, but when we're apart I'm someone else,
No problem neglecting my inner-self, so I can be placed high on your shelf,
To fit in, where I get in, once again, so that I'm cool and don't melt,

My image is all that I have, can't be too soft, or my people will laugh,
Can't be too smart, so I reject class, and trade my GED for a hood pass,
Just to have the imagery-that I perceived and gained from the streets,
To be one of the coolest niggaz, that anyone has ever seen,
And spray on fools like hair sheen, if they happen to say the wrong thing,
Impressing, whoever I'm with or whomever I tend to meet,
So that my image will be posterized before I end up deceased,

But constantly, my inside reminds me,
What's behind the glass that I choose not to be,
That what I'm representing, I'll end up resenting,
And this production I've created is in the wrong key,
But this is me, or is it? Am I truly official with it?
If I stood in a crowd, would I be obviously different?
Or would I be hard to find like Waldo?
And have the same shine as my friends, or my own glow?

Since I was taught at a young age, to perform on life's stage,
I can honestly say.....I...Don't....Know
Well until you know, stay on the road to find yourself,
So that the image you created was good for you and no one else,
Then you will truly be yourself.....

ReaLies

Open your eyes and tell me if you can truly see me,
Can you understand that I'm so real and in 3-D,
3 Dimensions, mind, body, and soul,
If my love you can handle, it's yours to hold,

Whether I move fast, or grind slow,
Sexual healing seems to be all that we know,
Never venture past the physical,
Like we're two bodies wrapped up in the unemotional,
Not ascending to higher heights, stuck in limbo,

Yet we so grown, but children in this game,
Ignorant to the fact that us wasting time is just a shame
Who's to blame? Don't want to point fingers,
So we choose to close our eyes, not see…
We sleep on love, like that's the way it's supposed to be,

When addressed we turn cold,
Showing each other stained glass and tinted windows,
So we can't see each other's 24kt. Gold,
Hidden treasure, foreign lands untold,
Just because our pride wouldn't let us grow,

But when we sleep, we dream something else will unfold,
So we rush to the fiction, since real life is no joke,
The dream is where we play, then where we stay,
Now that we're here, we like things this way,
Ignore the bitterness and stay with the sugar-coated candy,

And lay, eye's shut, avoiding the realness,
Dreams is what we all about now, who wouldn't
want to feel this,
Instead of work toward perfection, we pick
and choose our selection,
Who really cares anyway, most romance is in fiction,
Look at it this way and we create our own intervention,

Settle for this situation because without each other it's lonely,
So right now we cool with just each other only,
Even though we know this won't last forever; our fantasy,
Young and dumb steadily running from reality…

A Precious Item Overlooked

I met Martin Luther King Jr. yesterday,
Yes, I literally met him,
We spoke of his historic fight,
Without the use of deadly weapons.
Though he couldn't describe every second,
We shared most all his moments,
Was also there when he died,
And felt a special atonement.

Gandhi visited personally last week,
Mohandas, you may know the name,
We connected on all subjects of life,
And this week I'm not the same.
Socrates supplied epiphanies, I never dreamed
Using a philosophical approach,
Words so full of depth, carrying weight,
I'm still trying to break down his quotes.

I then shared a Peanut Butter & Jelly sandwich,
With none other than George Washington Carver,
We discussed topics on agriculture,
And how he made the south better farmers.
After lunch I picked up Winston Churchill,
Hard not to feel the strength he emits,
He taught on leadership, the significance of knowledge,
And of course a little politics.

Was placed in the middle of World War II,
After I watched the attack of Pearl Harbor,
Saw Jews, Germans, Hitler, FDR and Harry Truman,
Even the enlistment of both-my grandfathers.
I stood on the blood stained soil of Iwu Jima,
As the 6 men raised the national flag,
Behind Joe Rosenthal capturing the classic picture,
Not knowing the impression that image would have.

Right over the grass, I lifted off with the Wright Brothers,
Who taught me thoroughly about aerodynamics,
I also pointed out the glacier once more to Captain Edward Smith,
But I don't think my voice rose over the engines of the titanic.
I panicked the first few days I worked in Henry Ford's Model T plant
Seeing many crippled workers and laborers lose limbs,
So I went to study with Alfred Ely Beach, in NYC,
As we worked hard to develop the first Subway System.

Changed my dirty clothes on the border of New Orleans,
Stepping into the delivery room of Jazz,
Right off the Bayou, entering in by "sea-section,"
Was birthed holding a trumpet and sax.
Then I marched with an all Black Panther Party,
Lead by Huey P. Newton and Bobby Seal,
Working to empower African Americans,
And stop the mindset that caused us to kill.

Sat and chilled on the North & South Poles,
After I walked the equators imaginary line,
Went through the jungle examining curious creatures,
And struggled through an entire Mt. Everest climb.
Stood next to an erupting Hawaiian volcano,
Then cooled off under the Niagara Falls,
Passed tools to the sculptors working on Egyptian statues,
And observed Shah Jahan building the Taj Mahal.

I sharpened the pencil Walt Disney used to draw-
The first sketches of Mickey Mouse's face,
Then knelt behind Picasso's very own easel,
As I dipped his brush in mixed paint.
Was entertained by Leonardo Da Vinci,
The definition of a true Renaissance Man,
Showed me things on subjects far ahead of his time,
Proving anything is possible if you think you can.

Was behind the turn tables, mixing the first hip-hop record,
Then let DJ Kool Herc take the seat to teach,
Saw the entire transition in the lyrics of all music,
Converted Records, to A-tracks, then to Cassettes, CD's, and MP3's.
I was even present in Tupac's and Biggie's studio,
As they recorded multiple classic albums,
I saw the beef rise between the East and West coast,
And the drama that rose from the outcome.

I was in Hurricane Katrina, the California Earthquakes,
The lunar module, Neil Armstrong, landed 1st on the moon,
The Great Depression, the American Revolution,
And saw the first glimpse of the planet Neptune.
I was riding in the 61' Lincoln JFK was killed in,
Awoke at the Dawn of the Information Age,
Saw vividly the genocide taking place in Africa,
And stood under the monumental falling World Trades.

I dodged a hand grenade in Vietnam,
Explored the new frontier with Lewis and Clark,
Passed Thomas Jefferson the Declaration of Independence,
EQ'd Michael Jackson's "Thriller," before it soared off the charts.
Was in the dark before Edison gave us his light bulb,
Where I cut the tip of my finger on the Excalibur Sword,
Swore in the first African American President,
And closed my eyes full of tears as they crucified my Lord.

Now as I pour these events from my memory,
All, really, would be too much more to name,
I reflect on how I was given these opportunities,
It all came from an encounter with the most humble slave.
In chains, he lifted his head when he saw me,
His surprised face made me feel like I was unreal,
He reached out so that I would help him stand,
So with a firm grip, I assisted, lifting him to his heels.

Peering off into the distance, he pointed out at a rising new war,
That was namely Civil, but looked more like a gruesome show,
Our background was filled with the echoes of artillery,
So as we walked along, he stumbled, as bombs would explode.
I held my ear close as he nervously whispered,
Scared that someone in the distance would hear,
The last time he was caught sharing words of this nature,
The punishment he had received was severe.

But this issue he endeared, and his look was sincere,
Which lead him to continuously speak,
He spoke on an item that was currently unavailable to them,
That they cherished, but most now wouldn't seek.
Told of a bleak future he'd seen in nightmares,
Of those in the black race who'd stay enslaved,
But yet still held on to one optimistic dream,
That those willing would be freed from these chains.

Where those unwilling could no-longer blame,
Anyone for this type of captivity,
That would bring poverty, inflicted-ill-manners,
And pessimistic, closed-minded mentalities.
Though slave's opportunities had been short-lived,
They would indulge in the slightest chance,
It was just the feeling of gaining perception,
And the drive to, hopefully, one day, advance.

But in a trance they were meant to be kept,
So these servants wouldn't know how to succeed,
To stay in their place and produce for the masters,
And never attempt any other possibilities,
Though they equally shared lungs-inhaling the same air,
They were forced to believe they were 3/5 of a person,
Because a whole being, would not be controlled,
So over their eyes must remain this curtain.

That was certain to block all types of knowledge,
Any information, and formal education,
And even when these slaves would be freed,
They'd carry over this new adaptation.
Which would be an expensive priced inflation,
On a potentially strong-held sad life,
And to make this matter even worse,
These free slaves would think it's alright.

To be dark as night in the midst of their minds,
When they could be as bright as stars in the sky,
The stars, those captives had followed before, to safety,
But now, we're wasting the real reason they'd strive,
So this slave chose to edify, in the deep shadows of danger,
Revealing the most precious item that's been overlooked,
Placed it firmly in my hands, as his eyes damply glistened,
Saying to "never underestimate the value of an open book..."

Tears

I've heard that tears are words…
That the heart doesn't know how to say,
A language that communicates, genuine,
With intimate, irreplaceable sincerity,

Inherently connecting all human beings,
Through a silent understanding, concretely definitive,
So when terms escape us, an unlearned process occurs,
Releasing internal expressions in the most natural form,

Causing a broken heart to bleed clear,
Steers a lost soul to transparently pray,
Reveals love in the purest way, defenseless,
Or the joyous bliss of a hilarious laughing matter,

Spilling passionate batter into our anger, sadness or gladness,
Into our fears, cheers, and relentless persevering efforts,
The remains evaporate but not what their presence
commemorates,
The ability to remove the red tape, and let go, vulnerable,

Traveling along the outlines of perfectly curved cheeks,
They trail, to cleanse internal ail, never to linger,
Accepting wholly from whence they came,
without pity or judgment,
But with sentiment, through healing, only
the giver can get,

Falling from the optical slit, washing away old perceptions,
Through this cleanse, we're relieved, with peace as a reward,
For tears have all been chores the heart must work through,
So when it's all over, we can smile, after while, happily…

Grandpa

I heard someone say…"In all thy ways…
Acknowledge HIM, and HE shall direct thy path."
If you know us, it's somewhat of a tradition,
Before we each grab a plate or glass.
After amen, we expect a rich baritone voice,
To rise above all others, so often times, I would laugh.
Then later, I began to wonder about this whole practice,
That maybe that was the true after-taste that he wanted to last.

They say grandfathers may have silver on their head,
But more importantly…gold in their heart.
I agree, mainly because of these valuable internal treasures,
That they continually pass down and constantly impart.
Not always through words, but through integrity and great stature,
We look to them as the head of our living family tree.
If not because of their ability to lead and their immense confidence,
Then the reason alone, of passing the test of time, supersedes.

Grandparents are generally loved easily by grand kids,
For their consistent loving nature and their ability to believe…
That their grandchildren are some of the greatest people to touch earth,
Sometimes delaying themselves in discipline, but only when it's of need.
I'm not really sure how they got the free reign to whip us,
Being that we "technically" are not their direct child.
But when I was growing up, it was something about their presence,
That could calm us down, making us a little less wild.

That's why now, some parents, after they've lost total control,
Drop them off at their parents, and then…keep going.
Because these season vet's have a special way of nurturing their seed,
A secret some go through life without ever knowing.
Grandfathers seem to have their own frequency with grandsons,
A connection that reminds me of a remote-starter.
Just knowing that they sit in the audience as we perform,
Is a boost of adrenaline that makes us try a little harder.

And granddaughters are princesses that can do no wrong,
Can talk their way out of everything, and ask for anything.
So often times when fathers have irresponsibly dropped the ball,
They are the manly example used, and who they view as their king.
And these things I've seen, as the grandchild of one,
Who's name is as legendary as the Big London Clock.
Ben, more formally, Benjamin, the only grandfather I've known,
And I can say that I'm glad he's the one that I've got.

The last of his family, so just maybe God saved the best,
His song was "God Speaks," through him, maybe we heard what God said.
And I believe that I can speak for every grandchild in the room,
When I sincerely say the words, "We Love You Granddad…."

The Approach

Umm…Excuse me young lady, do you have a second maybe,
Just so I can tell you, when I saw you, you impressed me greatly.
And I hope the way that you walk, will align with the way that you talk,
Cuz I would truly hate me taking this time to stop, was for naught.

But on a note we call another, do you have a significant other?
If you do, it's unfortunate, but man…that's one lucky brutha.
You said no? aight coo, didn't wanna just walk off like a fool,
Even then, the chance for us to speak, for that, I would've been greatful.

I'm lovin all of your details, from your curly hair all the way to your nails,
Your attractiveness came over me like a spell….and well,
Made me come out of my shell.

I see you're made up of perfect dimensions,
Which I wouldn't mind showin further attention.
No disrespect and please don't neglect, I only approach
  with the best intentions.

And please don't get me confused, with some of these dudes,
Who feel as if they have something to prove.
I only want the opportunity to do, things to-and-for
  you no otha could eva do,
Like respect, protect, and often-times spoil you, so I could be who,
You eventually stay loyal to.

Find out what makes you laugh, mad, and even all of your interests,
And be fascinated by the time that you're finished.
Because personality is what truly matters to me, the rest will fade away,
And slowly begin to cease.

So may I have the combination to your safe,
  so you can open up and reveal your treasure case.
Cuz my intent is more than just spittin game and things,
With you, I only visualize myself, approaching a queen….

Unprepared Creator

Spread bout as wide as the ocean, bout as damp as the sea,
Lust is feelin' so good, like a hot summer's day breeze.
The volcano is wakin', the heat constantly risin',
The pain is feelin' so good, so happy, tears comin' down cryin'.

Convicting feelings now faded, impressive results from this situation,
The two ignorant to the fact that they're making a new creation.
Wasn't really prepared for this, sparked by the anticipation,
Deep in what some may call love, other's see as temptation.

Dazed-they slowly come to an end, can't wait to start reminiscing,
But found a piece of the puzzle they started was shockingly missing.
Confirmations now leading to doubt....then worry.....now fear,
Regretting all of the steps that drove them to this point here.

Was told to think nothing of it, doubt anything serious happens,
Unable to take his word for it, takes test...sees positive in the caption.
Tears return once again, because of the new circumstances,
Barely thought about, let alone evaluating the slim chances.

Was taught that-that was romance, sharing this gem with another,
But when the news was voiced, found he was a part-time lover.
Had no plans to stick around, had already begun to move on,
This critical time in one's life, she now shares all alone.

Finds a way to be strong, since destruction's not in her nature,
Is lookin' for ways to forgive, not wanting to end up a hater.
Questions thought to be answered, now leads to confusion,
The love that was once pursued, disguised and viewed as intrusion.

Was thought to be given freely, by the words that were spoken,
But just like that carnival ride, she had paid for her token.
Because 6 words, he said, convinced her she should,
They're familiar, they go..."if you loved me, you would".....

Fish for Me

What are you telling me dude,
This is food for my soul?
I ate this morning already,
And I'm pretty full-yo,
Truthfully I'm only here because I'm tryna get this girl,
And to go further, I got to experience a piece of "her world,"

To bad I'm not planning on her being in my future……

My bad, keep zoning out, let me try and listen,
Don't really understand, so like in school,
He's losing my attention,
Saying that this one man died for us,
Trust,
I've seen a lot of that,
We just pour out a little liquor,
Ain't praised one of them yet,

But now he's more than a man,
And he died, just to then rise,
So is he coming or going?
I ain't come to hear lies,
After life? I doubt,
I visited my man's grave on his birthday,
And surprise-surprise his tombstone was still in place,

You say you have so much fun being a Christian,
What, to go to church everyday, pay,
Visit sick, and start missions,
O that's fun, try having 2 girls at once,
Roll blunts, and get drunk,
You see some of the funniest stuff,
When you gone off that skunk,

Dance with girls, then rock they world,
Chill with the homies, and bang yo sounds,
House parties be cool,
When we don't end up beating someone down,

And protection I got,
So I don't need to pray,
And from what I heard from ol girl,
You got jacked the other day,
And see that we don't play,

But you say forgive and forget,
Forgive? That's quite unlikely,
And we don't forget shhhhh.....
Yea that baby needs to be quiet,
And you...you...and you could get on a diet,

But whatever, we bout to be gone in a minute,
I'm at the point where this guy really needs to finish,
Wait, wait, you say you so blessed, it's embarrassing,
Wow, I ain't ever been a fan of people laughing at me,
But that's a clue to me that you don't really mess with the streets,
Cuz what you don't know is,
We all tryna get taken seriously,

Aight-cool-we standing,
What, you say my sins is burning?
I don't know about that,
But it's obvious yo a/c ain't working,
If you really want to see a burner,
Walk with me to the trunk,
Not even that far; most times I got one on tuck,

Man you still talking?
You ain't done yet?
Ay playa, no offense,
I think they got-bout all they gone get,
How do ya'll do this all the time?
Just look and listen,
You hear this brutha?
He sending ya'll MEN fishing,

Ha-ha….well my bad ya'll,
I missed the bait,
Get saved? Join ya'll?
Naaaaah, I'm straight,
Besides you telling these people you tryna get your members back,
You don't know why they missing?
Even I can see that,

So let me tell ya preacha preacha,
Before I leave,
You just lost another brutha,
Cuz you couldn't relate to me…..

You couldn't display to me,
Why this is somethin', I need
I heard these clichés,
and similes,
But all these metaphors,
Didn't open doors,

So why would I want to hear more,
I gave you my time,
One chance,
And it seems you missed the opportunity,
To change my current stance…

Special Forces

From Generals down to Cadets,
Spoke the oath to serve and protect,
Never fret in the face of the unlikely,
Confident to stand strong-backing down to nobody,

Proudly serving the people and the country-they stand for,
From shore to shore locking the violence back door,
So we can shop at stores, lemonade stand pour,
And watch players score; safely-

Yet at a steady pace we…
Walk past these individuals and easily ignore,
Or complain about how much they need to do more,

While they fight till they're sore,
In street and overseas wars,
They're the floor containing the underground evils,
That could penetrate our core,

Though not perfect,
Their efforts are worth it,
How much-worse it-would be,
If no one volunteered to do-the…
Job that keeps each and everyone of us free,

So I applaud…the one's…
Truly committed to clean up our streets,
So on to the next generation we'll teach,
To support military,
And not hate police…..

I Am A Man

M…A…N…three letters combining to create a small word,
A word that embodies immeasurable possibilities,
With strength to look at, what some called limits, absurd,
And push past boundaries like he knows no captivity.

An ageless marvel of power with no need of electricity,
So there's no use for memory upgrades and technical updates,
He only upgrades with wisdom and knowledge placed in his memory,
Which then makes him electric in his own unique way.

With available lustrous headlights, to make bleak paths, seem bright,
So his faith relates to a line of torches burning in a cellar of doom,
Though playfully some joke around with the term
known as "Shining Knight,"
When darkness of night had engulfed him, he still found
himself on the shining moon.

Finding a fascination in something that was outside of this world,
Since he was fearfully and wonderfully made in the image of
someone who is,
Though earthly troubles may hurl themselves upon him,
bringing tears impearled,
He can always lift his eyes to the hills for a source of heavenly bliss.

His name surely fits the definition of a naturally destined leader,
Having courage, tenacity, resilience, and unknown mental capacity,
Carrying his morals and character on shoulders even as waters gets deeper,
Not letting his integrity drown at the sight of a wave bringing tragedy.

No one can match the potency placed in his flavor of love,
So strong the lord put "wo" in front of man, to identify his mate,
Though containing a muscular frame, he can be as gentle as a dove,
To make whoever is under his wings feel undeniably safe.

No acting as he commits faithfully, loyalty attaches him stead-fast,
To everyone that he loves, anything that he does, and
whatever he chooses to say,
Steadily improving himself for the future, presently, building off the past,
So even though tomorrow is not promised, he's prepared
to face every new day.

Initiating, knowing that procrastination is a waste of
talent and valuable time,
Confident in his gifts, as he walks hot coals, to eliminate cold feet,
Using fear as running shoes, rather than a shield to hide behind,
Since his passion fights through risks, making the taste of victory sweet.

A savor boys can not experience, because they rarely
withstanding the test of time,
As ignorance blinds their eyes, and foolishness aids their immaturity,
Daily losing control of themselves, living with just the
tangibles on their mind,
Breeding jealousy, anger, lustful activities, and constant insecurities.

Complexes of superiority or inferiority tell them they have
something more to prove,
When really it turns into something to lose, as more fall by the wayside,
Many males view themselves as men, but are really
just children in adult shoes,
And we see them too often running from home, like
their attempting a first base slide.

But they must realize, when he was a child, he spoke and
understood as a child,
He thought as a child, but only after childish things were put away,
did he become man,
Not putting childish ones down, by pressuring abortion,
Abandoning, and imparting mental bile,
So let these boys not leave behind obligations like its
something that's easily outran.

Instead let him run from lying, cheating, stealing, and disrespect,
Leave behind verbal and physical abuse, and all types
of unnecessary violence,
Put down stupidity and disregarding knowledge, and
chase a higher intellect,
And put away all unwise remarks,
Often the most profound things are received in silence.

Though he'll always have the make-up of a king, he's still
one that's chosen to serve,
Made to give, created to work, invent, conceive and to discover,
An entity that not only creates life, but was also put
here to help preserve,
So when he finds someone that resembles his qualities,
he can easily call him brother.

Creating a bond stronger than all others, then reaching back to assist more,
Because men should be true role modes, like lighthouses
for young boys to see,
Leading their unstable mentalities to a more solid continental shore,
Remembering he was not an island, nor should any other one attempt to be.

Making him no longer constrained to these stereotyped limits,
If he has received his purpose, envisioning success, he shall surely win,
Having a mixture of majestic potential,
Plus the blood-sweat-and tears of extraordinary descendents.
So that he can hold his head high, saying…"I AM A M…A…N…"

Broken

I'm wishing on a star, that someone will take me away from all this pain,
Some place afar, where the days are bright, not clouded with rain,
Where I can hold my head high and realize that I'm needed,
And not easily walked by, shunned, shown no love, and mistreated,

I'm constantly ignored and I really hate this feeling,
It's like being in a room of locked doors, and on an island sits this building,
And when I'm finally acknowledged, no one listen's to my voice,
They say my thoughts are unpolished, so they turn me off like white noise,

So a loner I've been, I am, and plan to stay,
Since people barely ever grin when they see me walking their way,
I swim in the sewers of life, since I'm valued as much as their waste,
As my thoughts become filled with more strife-I cannot
hold myself *together,*

I obviously lack the proper paste...

An improper pace for life's race seemingly gets one nowhere,
Too high are the stakes, with short arms reaching for the highest
shelf on a broken chair,
So I sit by myself, considering all the exits,
Since my entrance was unexpected, and my
existence constantly unaccepted,

Do you think if I left that anyone would care?
They haven't seen me on this island's crest, their jets too
high to notice my flare,
At least then I would be able to feel less misery,
No longer meditating on anything, because I gained invisibility,

But how easily I would veer from this path if someone showed love to me...

But my wish on that star brought nothing but a chance for me to reflect,
It's not about how it is given, but more about how I handle neglect,
While I was waiting for someone to give me love,
Over myself, I placed everyone above,

And until I could like myself, I should expect nothing from anyone else,
So the only option I saw vividly was death,
Not that I was made for a purpose,
Its difficult being at your best, when you feel that your life is worthless,

Because misery loves company, without company, it
overwhelms, then subdues,
But with life you're given one thing constantly, the ability to choose,
So please don't decide to give up on yourself, because
we're all made for a reason,
And you opting to destroy your life ,
Transpires as cutting the tree down before harvest season....

Is Hip Hop Dead?

It's been said, that Hip-Hop is dead,
Killed by tainted rap hits that were placed on its head,
Filled with poisonous lead, from gangster's bullets,
Thrown in vibrating trunks, while people turn heads,
Won't snitch to the FED's, **F**uture **E**mcee **D**elinquents,
Hungry for bread, instead sip on this KEG,
Killa's **E**ntice for **G**reed, brought Hip-Hop to its knees,
Shaken up by the jab that caused its slow-leaking nose-bleed,
And rap setup the greet, which was a set-up from the meet,
While a few white men got paid, just to sit back and oversee,
And the killa's entice just smiles, with fresh ganja between teeth,
And sprinkles a few ashes on the plate Hip-Hop had prepared to eat,
Duct-taped its mouth, hands and feet, but never closed its eyes to see,
How his reign on the music game would inevitably come to be,
Since he's in it for the money, let's only bring in gangstas and thugs,
Keep Hip-Hop on the side while he stops to sell drugs,
Let's pop off a few slugs at the bruh's tryna intercept,
Keeps Hip-Hop reloading them techs wearin its new bullet-proof vest,
Let's say these killas caught a few hot ones, hip-hop knew it wasn't true,
But since they kept the public convinced, it was little Hip-Hop could do,
Show-and-prove was Hip-Hop's model, show-and tell was
the slogan they used,
Now lets start this after party and go dumb off this krunk-juice,
Keep Hip-Hop sprung off this "X," takin pills from our generation,
Caused it to look at visiting girls with only sexual appreciation,
Watched them shake they a$* for Hip-Hop, in their scant wardrobe,
So it was hard for Hip-Hop not to call them b*t*hes and h**s,
That's the persona that was received, when watching the new videos,
Then sadly hung its head when the title was accepted like a golden globe,
It watched the killas entice bring in his feigns,
Addicted to the potent redundancy of unoriginality,
And as he sat down to eat, consuming unnecessary volumes of beef,
Ate it raw in front of Hip-Hop so it was always bloody,
Hip-Hop remembered those meals, but most were cooked till well-done,
After Hip-Hop's digestion, was barely any harm ever done,
But hip-hop watched these killa's sons, influenced off these entrées,
Disappointed at the newcomers paving this dark pathway,
Telling lies about what they got, Hip-Hop knows whose really getting paid,
And with every new advance was an advance towards hip-hop's mayday,

Far from hip-hop's heyday,
When its partners cared about music, not just create it with nothing to say,
While this KEG keeps it locked up, it has to learn some dance moves,
But these plates of "one-hit wonder-"bread aren't a source of "feeling" food,
Everyday hip-hop is beat up on in this upstairs empty room,
By a new fool acting hard using tactics on hip-hop to prove,
Hip-hop takes it like a man though, never forgot and always knew,
If a kat was really real, it would be seen in what that kat do,
But no matter how much hip-hop was hit,
It knew that "U Can't Touch This,"
One day the "Elevator" would come to bring it back to the "ATLiens"
Pick them up and come back cuz "Momma Said Knock You Out,"
Showing them what it's like to be called a "Rebel Of The Underground,"
Without using "Word Of Mouf", just picking up that "One Mic,"
To give these new kats "The Message" so you could "Fight For Your Right,"
"It's Tricky" knowing "The Bridge Is Over" still messing with "O.P.P."
But since these "Shook Ones" just know to "Push It," it's "Killing Me Softly,"
"People Everyday" grinding to keep chasing this "C.R.E.A.M.,"
Hip-hop started off doing this for free telling dudes
          "Don't Sweat The Technique,"
It was here for the "Rappers Delight" and to make the "Planet Rock,"
Didn't ever wait for nobody whether they were "Ready Or Not,"
Hip-hop wanted to help "Little Ghetto Boys" go from
          "The Project" to "The City,"
But they kept yellin back to hip-hop the "Mind Playing Tricks On Me!"
So no more fair fighting, won't "Put Your Hands Where My Eyes Can See,"
Since up-incomers had "Hell On Earth", they all stuff "Heataz" in they jeans,
Just some "Natural Born Killaz" that continually "Fight The Power,"
And hoping they "Find Ya Wealth", before it's their "Final Hour",
Still hip-hop hopes these "Niggaz 4 Life" will just "Walk This Way,"
To finally be able to sincerely say that "It Was A Good Day,"
Still reaching out to tell these rappers saying "I Know You Got Soul,"
So we can make "Dear Mama" glad her son's not at the "Crossroads,"
Hip-hop still fought no matter the "Changes" after cool Clive Campbell,
So hip-hop still lies in that room with "Street Dreams" in its head,
With this Killa's entice still in its house that has left it for dead,
But a few real ones have crept in to breathe in hip-hop, living breath,
The life-support that keeps it from its fast approaching death,
Since it's so much division, it's hard to make a pro-vision,

They used to want to make it out, not just enjoy their realism,
Hip-hop remembers them telling it like it is, writing public street-letters,
But did what they had to, to hopefully enjoy the sweet taste of better,
But hip-hop just lies, not at all dead, but with closed eyes,
Waiting for its alarm clock to go off at the right time,
Maybe that'll happen when emcees put positivity in their rhymes,
Instead of just having good hooks, will add good verses with real lines,
Not just to collect a check from which some rich white men sign,
Have a thought of the future without just having money on ya mind,
Because I believe hip-hop would love to see more of this kind,
From the heart, to the head, out the mouth, painting
beautiful pictures for ignorant eyes,
And watch true hip-hop arise from our "U.N.I.T.Y"

No Show

What I have is worth having,
Worth taking, experiencing, and grabbing
....holding, and keeps you continually longing for,
So all else that seems attractive, you'd then probably ignore,

It's greatness unexplainable, and so perfect it's unattainable,
The miraculous situations deliver unrealistically as dreamed up in fables,
With this, there's no stopping you, puts power behind
your thoughts to follow through,
Anything imaginable, it gives you the ability to now do,

For its test you're given the strength to complete, and the answers,
Pushing you, always propelling forwards never backwards,
When finished, you're then rewarded,
Feelings uncompared, trying to play back what your mind recorded,

But I have it; it's worth experiencing and grabbing,
But I won't show you, unlike the underwear of pants that are sagging,
It's worth taking, but since I don't share,
How can I expect you to believe my words are sincere?

From the outside looking in, it's just my interpretation,
Just words without action, similar to flirtation,
With fear of rejection, I keep this wonder to myself;
A lonely vacation,

This beautiful thing, I never put on display,
Never offering to anyone, the missing platter on my tray,
All because the risk of standing out to get shot down,
Lurks in my mind when others are around,

So on the ground I will stay, simply because I'm ashamed,
Knowing the one's in the spotlight occupy nothing compared to me,
But since I choose not to advertise,
Its unseen unique presence, will still be my worthless prize,

Because no matter how much I think it's worth,
Everyone blind to this fact, will never be fully immersed,
Hopes are just illusions inside of a secretive box
If no one ever sees what it is that you've really got....

Indecent Indulging

Improper thoughts of an object I see,
As I watch-longing for it-impatiently,
Trying to take ownership, like it was made for me,
And if it belongs to another, I look jealously.

In your presence, I acknowledge your beauty-embellishing,
So I take advantage of your image, visually,
Then use you for my satisfaction, mentally,
To experience the simulated feelings, emotionally.

And until I can have you, you're locked in my memory,
Like an invaluable-kept in a treasury,
Because your main purpose is for my pleasuring,
This is never enough, so there's no measuring.

You're my main aim, what I'm carefully triggering,
And if I must, I will resort to trickery,
Though when I see you, a treat, I get instantly,
Enriching, like an orchestral symphony.

This infatuation is the propeller of my submarine,
Pushing through the waters of my morals that keep resisting,
Ignoring my conscience, I move on, steadily persisting,
Because it holds my attention, it's ever-so interesting.

The side-effects of my addiction, may appear startling,
Some have even gone to call it frightening,
I call it the art of a connoisseur, dedicated to compiling,
It just so happens that my collection is demoralizing.

A poisonous pill that descends slowly, after swallowing,
But the after affects can come very quickly following,
A thought, that brought a mindset, till a desire is borrowing-
Every trustworthy conviction I had, and now towering.

It was escorted in, then began overpowering,
So all I can do now is comply to this attractively strong calling,
Though it's hard to see that with each step closer-I'm constantly falling,
As it takes me further than I'd go, on my own inclining.

This addiction- it captivates, this temptation-is so enticing,
This "love," has me paying the most expensive pricing,
So instead it is "lust" in my descent, I pictured as flying,
Even if this goal is scored, I…to myself, was lying.

Because I lost my decency in my committed prying,
To seek out this figurine and disregard my soul dying,
Because this lust only concerned my flesh satisfying,
And not my entire being, which I had isolated, undermining.

With all this effort I relentlessly chased, while my heart was crying,
That reality would never present what I had been fantasizing,
And I found out when I finally got it, that though it may be appetizing,
That I had stooped to a level so low, for just a small piece, not
even the whole thing…

I Have One

I have one…
Not two, just one…
One that stayed,
And one that strayed,

One that was brave,
Choosing to tackle this maze,
While one tossed me away,
And ran from this mistake,

Though two moved as one,
In the dark of the day,
Laid…in the heat of the night,
To erratically, procreate,

An unthinkable fate,
When two irresponsibly mate,
A combination that tends to make,
Someone born to complicate,

Then like a shockwave touching two,
I fazed one, and dazed one,
Though one was gone by my day one,
And missed my whole phase one,

Saw his face during phase two,
But that was quickly erased too,
Heard a "rolling stone" was how that one moved,
My relation to a rock, I never knew,

My young mind didn't grasp that view,
Until I began taking that formation too,
Growing incomplete with half my roots,
Since one side dipped like fondue,

A stereotyped manuscript I was issued,
While placed in the middle of two's issues,
Shot out in a role of a bastard,
That couldn't penetrate his Ol' Dude,

At the sight of his face, no feelings accrued,
When the 1 in my age sat before the 2, (12)
Since my guardian, one wasn't attached to,
I never had the chance to connect with you,

Without shoe's to step into,
I created my own, skipping curfews,
Since one was working days and nights through,
Providing for two, simply trying to make-do,

Her main focus struggling with men, bills, and food,
Kept me on the sideline, peripherally viewed,
Leaving me with the feeling of priority two,
That label hurt me more than anyone ever knew,

So like learning to tie a tie, and lace up my shoes,
I took things into my own hands, ignoring both of you,
Which consistently added more to her grievance,
Since my independence was driven misconstrued,

And often times she needed assistance,
Since one barely ever made an entrance,
One's division worked as a hindrance,
With our overflowing gap of distance,

I didn't cope with trying to forgive,
One's absence showed no repentance,
My manhood had constant resistance,
While my mind was wrestling relentless…ly,

Coping with the fact that I vividly see,
One + one made a disconnecting three,
A mother, a broken son, and a mystery,
Since the last one had "stranger-like" tendencies,

Never appearing to have general inquires,
Of whom I was, am, or would grow to be,
So, on the world I took out my misery,
Because my two examples didn't suffice equally,

So I have one…………..ME,
The only one that could never leave,
Countless splitting roads, and would never weave,
The only true relative I've seen,

Avoided glimpsing into glass frames,
Because our resemblance is deranged,
Without a spot in your center or focal length,
Mirrors just magnified my pain,

So I searched inside for my strength,
Though broken, I found a way to say, "I'm straight,"
Since one couldn't or wouldn't motivate,
Regulate, or at the very least…participate,

So I'm doing me, like I chose to masturbate,
And I only say that because I learned the "hard" way,
Difficult to manipulate as through life I mutate,
Into a person with dirt surroundings, that chose to elevate,

So I'll start with one moment,
One that I chose to change,
Starting with one decision,
One target, I'll fixate on in my brain,

To be the very best that I can,
Although my start wasn't sweet as sugarcane,
Because I only have One Life, One Future,
And on No ONE else will that responsibility remain…

...Let me be your poet tonight...

Let me be your poet tonight…

To grace your internal walls,
Walk your halls the write way,
And inspire you to break traditional laws,

Like gauze, let my essence rap you up,
As your emotions drink from my cup…
Of loving wisdom…this precision…
Penetrating deep like scalpel incisions,

Taste my realism
Savoring it's potent effects,

As my solid concepts…
…reveal my erect…

…Dic.tation…
From your preparation,
Extending rare invitations,
To feel unique sensations,

Like allies, aligning two continents,
Your ocean lies…between rhyming consonance,
Appreciating artistic confidence,
Metaphors supplying the softest kiss,

Let this poet's…temperance,
Fulfill your deepest fantasy,
Similes moving romantically,
Making you shake…rhythmically,

Taking every iambic meter of me,
Since tonight inches are less deep,
So let my lyrical scribes seep,
As my pen strokes your mentalities,

Let your short breath…breathe…
…my unlocking keys,
Openly setting you free,
Optimistically…

An emotional release,
As my utensil touches the pad,

So as my ink spills...
Your soul can climax,

Then go back…to reminisce,
About how proper poetics,
Made you feel that one night,
When your hunger was eclectic,

Then perfected…appeased by advice,
From a poet…out of sight,
Who waits steadily with his pen,
To always give it to you write…

MURDER

I grabbed the strap, and got my chicken on-
Meaning I cocked that,
Placed a knife in its sheaf,
Incase I need to slice me a piece,
The brass knuckles are comin' along;
I may need to crumble some bones,
And anything else I can find,
To shorten a ni**a's life-time,

Because my mind placed me on-
An entirely different grind,
To proceed writing these cats off,
Like charity donations
And though I often times,
Probably need no participation,
I brought a few of my homies,
In case I need some translation,

Used to smooth over and clear up,
Anything I wasn't ready for,
Can't ever be off guard,
When you're in the midst of war,
Though I use the term war,
It's frequently 1 going against 4,
Having that n**a think he seein' quadruple,
When lookin' up from the floor,

And if he is, that's just 12 more-
People that he'll visualize,
Which will make it lil' easier
For us to stay unidentified,
In his eyes, are 16 masked men,
Like black-suited Alaskans,
Guns blazin' like gatlin's,
And he'll neva' outlast them,

And then on to the next,
Making moves like in the game of chess,
Having these pawns go out quickly,
If not wearing a vest,
Clearing these streets of the weak,
In these slums and projects,
So I'll give them that poison-
Their lungs will inject,

For a lil more respect,
I roll dice on lives-with no bet,
And even elderly and female,
I won't choose to neglect,
If they're in the way-
Of what I'm initially tryna get,
I'll peel more than one cap,
No Russian roulette,

What I interject,
Separates body from spirit,
And my power comes,
When I also see that you fear it,
Need no leader-to-cheer it,
I can ride Doe-low too,
Really makes no difference,
Since my subjects aren't bulletproof,

I have multiple types of equipment,
In case my clip wants to jam,
Instead of knowledge in college,
Stab wounds in your body, I'll cram,
Then scram, like I ran-
And hopped on any tram,
Leaving you faced down to "Seacrest,"
Like you been a Ryan fan,

But when I say see crest,
It symbolizes my hardness,
That shield's always with me,
Without wearing Teflon on my chest,
If you say I'm a hot mess,
I'll leave you wasted in mine,
If it bugs you, then fine,
I'll go and spray this pesticide,

And careless when you cry,
I'm taking you out your misery,
Since you lived like a b*t*h,
I'll watch you die, equally,
As a dog that was never able,
To outlast his fight,
But no teeth clinched your neck,
It was my hands held tight,

Watchin' another face turn pale,
And eyes start to dim,
Just one more body,
I left in their own blood to swim,
My worst case scenarios are bein' killed,
Or placed in the pen,
I fear neither, so either way,
In the end…I win,

Since I began, I felt a void,
So I put physical holes in others,
And my pains were never smothered,
Instead grew-undercover,
The hate, vengeful, madness-
Placed in every bullet in the chamber,
And every time I re-up,
I reloaded another dosage of anger…

Since my life is not my own,
But a vessel for the most evil,
At an early stage-I lost control,
When I made my first victim see-through,
Watch closely and shockingly,
My life flashed in front of them too,
Their pain displayed mine internally,
So their yells matched my soul's tune,

And I see every one of their faces,
When my eyes close to sleep,
It just happens to be a reminder,
Of the company I chose to keep,
The cold dark life of the dead,
Consistently lies in my bed,
Since I'm a dead man walkin',
When I rise instead,

And that's not because I've been known
To have a price on my head,
But because I act as if I feel nothing,
Like havin' skin made of lead,
Dead to emotions, gore, horror,
And these terror infested screams,
Dead to the prayers before death,
And the ending of early dreams,

Might have started off as protection,
Now I used it reinforcing,
That nothing that hurt me in the past,
Will do what I have foreseen,
So I beat everyone to the punch,
In this life of paranoia,
Smokin' all who I choose,
Like smog rising in California,

When actually I'm considered the weakest,
Of any type of person,
To take out my problems on everyone,
And still choose to worsen,
Our communities, societies,
And all forms of economies,
Acting selfishly as I decide to lay wait,
Preying on the weak,

The softest man becomes intimidating,
With the help of ammunition,
How hard would you be going up against-
The same level of competition
If everyone you approached,
Had the same feeling about you,
And you were the one on the ground,
Being stomped by 4 dudes,

You'd probably front like you don't care,
And act like you're unmoved,
When really your vulnerability,
Would shock you're whole crew,
Because despite your point of view,
Life doesn't start nor end with you,
You're as human as the person you killed,
And one day you'll die too,

And the arrival of that moment,
You'll realize the truth,
That death is just the beginning-
Of a longer, harder road,
In this world many inflict bodily harm,
Wanting to be feared the most,
But all real fear should truly belong,
To the one that can kill your soul…

Limitless

What if I could live my life like a king,
Then find me a queen, to truly share everything,
If I could head for the ceiling, without dodging the ceiling fans,
U know the people that want to cut you down,
when they see at the top you almost stand,

Matter fact...
Why is there even a ceiling,
Can't we have the feeling that we can make it out,
Despite our everyday living conditions,

What if I could be looked at as an individual,
Not a person representing a group of people everywhere I go,
If you could just listen to my voice, instead of the choir's tone,
Not judging me by my color and the streets that engulf my home,

What if I didn't have to listen to gunshots while I sleep,
Live in peace, instead of being happy I made it to see the next week,
Respect police, because I knew they'd be truly protecting me,
And not have them glad to see us clean our own selves off the streets,

What if the government told us honestly that they care for "we,"
And it showed because we all got treated equally,
Be sincere about giving everyone quality,
Instead, like in their pictures, giving us that government "cheese,"

What if I could go to court and get a fair trial,
Know that the truth was reached because of the oath and the bible,
The judge would show me love even if I resembled a thug,
And would really think about my life, not just sweep it under the rug,
When he looked through his glasses he'd see the potential in me,
And would understand my life is worth more than just a hard jail seat,

What if defeat wasn't an option and girls could love me
no matter what I bought them,
The women would already know to respect themselves,
And judge us men, inside alone, not by our
lacking or enhanced wealth,
We would respect our women, because they were meant to be,
Then cherish and love their position as our helpmeet,
Abortions wouldn't exist because people knew life was heaven sent,
Would no longer neglect it, but choose to value its preciousness,

What if I could love myself above everything else,
Be satisfied with me, not comparing myself to this world's filth,
Separate myself from the crowd, as far as east is to west,
Still know I'm the best that endured through every test...
Without feeling there was a need for people to be impressed,
And be who I want, do what I planned, while
holding integrity in my right hand...

"But you can," I heard in the distance,
"You can change every single thing that was listed,
My friend, you are looking from a narrow point of view,
I must say that I am a lot more optimistic than you,
You see, you only address negative circumstances,
Instead of noticing the positive chances,
The best things in life you'll one day see,
If you begin to look at things, spiritually..."

And that's where it ended, no more needed to be said,
And though the voice sounded quite distant,
felt as if it was in my head,
Then it was revealed to me, it was my inner man,
And with this new information, how could I not
take the right stand,

I would be the change that I never saw,
And not "wish" or "what-if" like with a crystal ball,
Stand tall and be glad to see, that eventually, I will make history,
Because I am a living legend with a new objective,
You ask, what can one man do? I answer, change his entire perspective...

MONEY MAN

I'm tryna get this money, gotta get cash,
So I can live the good life, not struggle like in the past,
When you got bread, you got options…some variety,
Because I'm tired of seeing the same thing day-to-day,
staying on repeat,

Mainly this is what we know, what we used to, no dough,
But not this brutha, see I'm constantly on the grind to get mo',
Seen all that it can get you, if you weren't before, it makes life smooth,
No more lonely days, bad times, and sad songs, singing the blues,

So that's my hustle, getting money no matter what,
Getting what I want and keeping everything that I touch,
Because I live for it, it's the heart at the center of my core,
Got so good at it, money I've learned to lure,

I breathe it like air; it's replaced my pupils and caused this stare,
Looking only at the path that will take me there,
My ears are the antennas that are picking up the signal,
Tracking this money keeps me on the fly-seeking like missiles,

My feet are the mode of transportation that takes me there the quickest,
No immunity whatsoever so that I can say I'm the sickest,
My mouth only speaks it, matter of fact,
And my hands are the glue that keeps it all in tact,

On it, I never turn my back, never get lazy with it or slack,
Remain doing it big my Nig., just like McDonald's Mac,
Understand that I'm made of money; money's my world, my life, my wife,
Being without it is so wrong, which ya'll know isn't ever right,

My mind is as smooth as the machines that print the money,
And my love for it is the power that keeps this phenomenon running,
Because the cash flow I'm in breeds power-you see,
And a powerful man…I intend to be, most definitely,

Then comes the priceless object, we all call respect,
And from the view I've seen, you no get, without…pro-fit,
I can fulfill all my wants and needs with this,
Be my own genie that granted each and every one wish,

Now that's what I call success, being able to get rich,
Satisfy every itch, and embellish in it,
Because money bought me friends, the ability to
live like a king, with gems,
It bought me drinks, a winning position, and someone to always listen,
It paid for this huge mansion, for me to mess with girls in pageants,
And a chariot to ride in, with on the exterior rims and tints,
It brought the limelight, with my protection always with me,
Popularity and a health plan if I ever happen to get sickly,

I stay fly because I can,
Everything now matches- shoes, shirt, hat and pants,
I now have a new stance, and it didn't all happen by chance,
I can now ride in elevators, as the cruise takes me to island sands,

Can chill whenever I like, and eat till my stomach feels right,
Receive tons of insight, and can do everything you
can't do in your lifetime…twice,
So why not love money, it's taken care of me so well,
I love speeding through life, and watch the rest of ya'll move like snails,

And I thought I was completely happy, well…untiiiil……………

I noticed I had riches and not wealth,
Money plus satisfying emotions was something I never felt,
I found I was made of money and sadly nothing else,
Because I had placed it too high above everything else,

I had paid for friends, but never gained loyalty,
And though I lived life like a king, never felt like royalty,
And my gems, which came as a surprise to me, didn't
contain the natural clarity,
Stayed with a drink, but it never quenched my thirst,
Had that winning position, without the satisfaction of being 1st,

Had someone who would listen, but couldn't right my wrongs,
And that mansion on the hill, was a crib to lay my head, not a home,
The model chicks didn't have any love for me,
And that chariot tinted out, still didn't provide privacy,
The limelight just kept all eyes on me….

The protection was always there, but I never felt safe,
And though I was popular, wasn't really ever great,
That heath plan was cool, but didn't give me true healing,
And though I stayed fly, I constantly knew I was under a ceiling,
My clothes kept me stylish, but didn't extend a warm feeling,

The stance kept me posted, but gave me nothing to stand for,
And yea, I rode the elevators, but was never delivered to the top floor,
I could chill and relax, but didn't really have peace,
Could eat till I was full, without it being a true feast,

The insight was alright, but I didn't receive real wisdom,
So I had a hard time when it came to making crucial decisions,
All to find that my love of money had gotten me nowhere,
Exterior without interior, it's like having no lungs, with tons of air,

So now I see why it's so lonely at the top,
Because climbing that latter, I never knew-my soul, I had dropped,
And my heart no longer contains the ability to beat,
Because I've placed a dollar bill where my heart used to be,

I fought that green giant, who, unlike David, I couldn't defeat,
Thinking it would transform my empty life, making it complete,
But when I reached this position I found that money answereth all things,
But if you crave it for the wrong reasons, you only get the answering machine....

Masquerade Party

Join me in a place, where we are not ourselves,
With mask affixed to our surface, like a reptile's scales,
Though it seems like a party, it's really more like our world
With these disguises tightly wrapped, to not become unfurled,

Causing us to act, speak, and live in this foreign attire,
With mind frames-like mainframes we chose to rewire,
As a machine, configured by the commands of my current mood,
I can be whatever I want to be for any moment that I choose,

...Except real, that's what we mimic and wish we could be,
But if I ever expel this mask, that ends this joyous festivity,
Since my happiness is based, deceivingly on a counterfeit rock,
Like a girl believing she received a diamond, when really its C-Z that she's got,

I keep a shield always in front of me and a cape that stays at my back,
The super-hero of my personality, saving me in areas that I lack,
This shield and cape cover all sides, leaving my feet exposed,
So I talk-the-talk, but won't walk-the-walk, I just hope you never pay close...

Attention...forcing me to overdose on this placebo prescription,
Stacking lies upon lies to sustain this recipe in my kitchen,
Which in turn, eventually serves up a plate of disaster,
But I can't see that far ahead, lacking the equipment of a forecaster,

Still I live for the moment, being who I think I should by the minute,
When I'm not hanging with you, I talk behind your back to others I've befriended,
I've ended all loyalty to others since I can't even commit to myself,
It's like I'm cheating on me, with a fictional character living in the same shell,

Becoming attached to the one you like, rather than the one in true life,
Trying to enjoy it, even while I have this festering internal strife,
It's like the tip-of-an-Iceberg, that you've never seen completely,
So I keep my responses generally vague, and rarely answer discretely,

Constantly being dishonest, for deception is the author of my manual code,
Telling you that I own it all, when really my creditors have control
Like dancers on a pole, they'd strip me of everything given the chance,
But that you don't need to know, while I keep up this front for my fans,

I stretch the truth like elastic waist bands, for the women I'm trying to get in,
I tell them that god is love, since we're in it, this can't possibly be sin,
So that I can win, or at least score, in my opinion, it's really the same,
Like a player of an athletic team, I'm out-hitting the shower, after I run game,

Cleaning myself of impurities-not cleansing my make-up of immaturity,
Because in these physical tangibles, I find my security,
Subsequently there's always a new item, so I change with the trends,
You'd be surprised at the plans, in my mind-behind a disguise full of grins,

I'll be the one-who comes around with an ulterior motive,
To enjoy your body, status, or money, appearing to be supportive,
My forgery is like sorcery, mystics I use to confuse,
When I've had my fill or when I'm discovered, on to the next subject-I'll move,

Like I'm dancing with various partners around the ballroom floor,
What remains is an impression that leaves their feelings and emotions sore,
I've had many tales behind backs, fitting the titles, rat, snake, or leach,
My shady white lies are now standing out like the obvious stains of bleach,

Though many reach for different names, it always dwindles down to one term,
"FAKE" the infestation of immorality that quickly spreads like germs,
The feeling, that you alone, are not enough, so you portray something you're not,
In masquerade parties…the mask'll-raid-your-body, causing you as a person to rot,

As a user, abuser, and all around loser, not investing in true relationships,
I fake it-to-make it, as a basic imitation, taking my place among true hypocrites,
Have my own version of the word unique, turned it to U-N-I-"K"?
Because without you, I'm not ok, irrelevance makes my total purpose go away,

My fictitious character only lives in the minds of the naive,
Until you smarten up and we "fall" out with you dropping me like "leaves,"
We all live out our character, but if you don't let the real one show,
Don't be surprised, it may get exposed, by these live audience episodes,

In front of no tape-deck rolls, but these memories still record it all,
Remembering the rise, all the way to the climax, but most importantly, the fall,
The ever-present lingering truth that there is a day, when I'll become unveiled,
And it's sad that what lies beneath, I won't ever recognize, until…………..

I no longer find the need to leach off others, and continually people please,
Penetrating deeply into fulfilling interaction, abandoning being a tease,
Because, I find, false identification to be like a robber in a service station,
You might hold it up just to get what you want, but it never fully restores your
deprivation,

You might use it to get what you need, but for more, you'll bleed,
Cutting yourself, trying to be own blood brother or sister, but you won't succeed,
Since the real you and the fake you are unfamiliar,you're still left confused,
The separation is so distinct; one can't donate blood for the other's to be transfused,

We should all grow to be viewed sitting in a muse, as antiques authenticated,
And not have white lies ashamed of our dark past, like Jim Crowe laws segregated,
For, when the day comes that you make it to the place that you've always wanted to be,
You don't want to say that the throne is lonely because you forgot to bring the real "me"…

Princess Cut

I heard her,
Cry out in agony
As I whip this creature-
Like an animal herder,
Acting as her trainer,
Steering her straight,
Keeping a tight leash,
On my b..i..t..c..h,

That's how I treat her,
In one of the worst ways,
And yet she still remains,
Like I told her to "stay,"
Cuz I play on her fears,
Leaving more than mascara smears,
And the pain I inflict,
Strongly inclines her to adhere,

Like the bottle of a good year,
This "fine" one knows me as her container,
And if her cork shoots off at the mouth,
My fist lies against her teeth like retainers,
Fixing the issue once again,
Covering wounds with band-aids,
Skin stained with the colors of Kool-Aid,
Mixes of cherry, blue-berry, and grape,

And sadly I savor the taste,
As badly flavored as it is,
Even worse-looking on at this "punch,"
Are teary eyes of our kids,
Hoping their minds are unreceptive,
Though there's an underlying truth,
That along with their mother's body,
I leave their memories bruised,

Anger educed this stranger,
Who's my identical twin,
And though she calls this love,
It's pain we keep putting her in,
When he steps off, I'm back again,
Stepping in to switch it back up,
Handing her princess-cuts,
But leaving this princess…cut,

Armor shines dull on this knight,
Let the light from the stones bend,
They'll act as her best friend,
So when I discipline, they'll mend,
Neva been controlling or crazy,
But all these women aren't ladies,
Won't let her words penetrate me,
When she's trying hard to break me,

Continually she mistakes me,
As some soft dude, acting brand new,
So since you talking like a nigga,
Let's see you fight like one too,
I hit her hard with a 1-2,
Like I'm doing a sound-stage mic-check,
Since my feelings, she sometimes neglects,
With her blatant disrespect,

My intellect-not quite as quick,
So as she leads this argument,
My sentences become thin,
While hunger for vengeance grows thick,
It's thick and thin, which I'm in the midst,
When verbal abuse springs from her lips,
Attacking my ego-driven manliness,
And I find myself starting to drift,

Often times, have I walked away,
Acting as a prey in this chase,
Till I'm bait, backed in a corner,
And took it out on her face,
Placing my morals and manners aside,
To revive remnants of my pride,
Causing your pain to be external,
While mine had formed inside,

I've tried getting past my memories,
And rough things that I've been through,
But when the pain won't subside,
I visualize cross hairs in my view,
So I make you carry this cross,
With a limped walk, and a muffled talk,
Since I "socked," like no shoes,
Breaking rules I may have been taught,

To keep my twin arising,
When I continually sink,
With a blink of an eye, I react,
Without taking the time to think,
The weakest link, when under pressure,
Because my chain has a kink,
Keeps me in circles, like roller rinks,
And dead to her, like her new fur's mink,

With my feelings out of sync,
I'm constantly pushed past my brink,
Watching my control go extinct,
Faster than an eye can wink,
…So think, who's really the hoe?
If by your anger you're controlled,
Making you fold into a position,
Like your b..i..t..c..h, would go,

It's a missionary, that's very scary,
When she lies-crushed, like wine berries,
Making her tarry in this unsafe place,
But her love for you won't let her walk away,
Strength that was made to protect,
Used with no respect, cuz you're hurt,
One of the most precious things on earth,
You hit on, like football turf,

And with every hit you make,
You always seem to fumble her away,
Lost to separate, house restraint,
Or dead to the beatings-if she stays,
Because a grown man can't behave,
Instead have to hand raise,
Are you brave if you fight your mate-
Whose frame sits in a glass case?

A failing race in which you run,
When your body displays the sign "In Use,"
Helpless to the bondage of your feelings,
Lead to this inexcusable domestic abuse,
Leaving you with feeling of guilt and regret,
Since your image of love overshadows your respect,
When really, as men, we never separate those two terms,
A Man you may not be, but it's never too late to learn…

My Destiny, My Fate

I was born the first of three,
But we all entered simultaneously,
Delivered as one, taking my first breath,
While two also breathed, resembling me,
One held these two shiny keys,
Labeled "Consequences" and "Endless Opportunities"
The other just watched with penetrating eyes,
A pen in hand, writing mysterious calligraphies,
The author's name was signed Destiny,
The other, known as Fate, held both keys,
I often wondered where they were from,
And who appointed their activities,
Their intake was of different cuisine,
Feeding off my thoughts and words, and savoring my dreams,
On top of that, devouring my actions,
Even if some of the remains were obscene,
They stayed in reverberated redundancies,
Destiny loved to write, Fate loved to lead,
Destiny aged faster, seeming to grow wiser,
While fate developed with me, moving more spontaneously….

Seemed, that wherever I moved, Fate already knew,
Even on occasions when I had extended no clue,
So whether I made a choice of greater or less quality,
Fate, would glance at Destiny, weigh both keys, and then choose,
Either the equivalent repercussions, or privileges to walk through,
Though in the midst of my actions, the aftermath, I rarely knew,
So when I made educated decisions, or chose with a clouded vision,
I noticed Destiny would come in or further out of my view,
Working on my behalf, though we've not yet been introduced,
Making me start to think they know me better than I do,
Which has me slightly confused, since they seem to decide nothing,
As they automatically place my foot into the fitting shoe,
Time was named the agent that these shoes were loaned through,
Though this loaner was sneaking-ly short, it was there for my use,
The three of them worked together, and I often times felt left out,
But, I noticed they all contained controller slots marked "YOU,"
Ignoring it-Fate lead me to trust in love, who hurt me too,
Then slowly I found in life, that time heals all wounds,
And once healed, I broke rules, leaving the potion steadily spilled,
Because my run-in with love left me at the slightest, un-amused,

I then saw a fuse attached to the bottom of time's feet,
At about the same moment I noticed my life was in full speed,
Fate was still there, unlocking doors for me to openly walk through,
But the key "Endless Opportunities", was used far less frequently,
And with every door that opened, I moved closer to this Destiny,
So close, to the point that it stopped writing; like it was about to speak,
It stood, shaking its head, and without a word pointed to my rear,
And when I had turned to look, I saw someone named Legacy,
They proceeded, telling me, that they had been my parallel multitude,
My Destiny, My Fate, My Legacy, and My Time too,
But Legacy only utters words from a legendary story,
And since my plot never improved, mine was forced to stay mute,
That's when my loaner stepped in, revealing the end of its fuse,
Meaning my time was completely up, and that's how it eventually blew,
As I lay, my character arose, and attempted to try and stay,
But while searching, it vividly recognized who it stumbled into,
And when we locked eyes that day, I knew I had met my Fate,
Who only told me it was over, and that I had been a little too late,
That my grave would stay closed, so I wouldn't be allowed escape,
Since I made the mistake of living a life, I chose not to regulate...

Last Shot

If I was caught in the midst of my last ***shot***,
Where would it be?
In the bottom of a small glass, the tip of a syringe,
Or in the chamber of a nickel-plated 9-piece,

Would it be aimed at my enemy's head,
Or would that needle penetrate my veins,
Or would that glass be coated with something that taste like tequila,
But looks like rain?

Burning my esophagus on the way down,
Just to temporarily ease my brain,
Causing me to act in another reality,
And switch to an entirely different mind frame,

So what could've been done with positive thinking,
Instead is handled with profuse drinking,
Just to say "Hey, it was another fly weekend,"
But my story has dark spots, like your eyes when blinking,

Meaning a lot of flashes just pieced together,
Placing mental gaps on the procedure taken that night,
Until I saw the snapshots from a friend,
My a.k.a. photographer on-sight,

Fried, with that last ***shot*** pushing me over the edge,
And if that night I came up dead,
With a slurred speech, reeking of alcohol, as I knelt and bowed my head,
What do you think The Lord would've said?

Maybe if I was seated in my home, all alone,
Behind a closed door, on my bed,
Sterilizing this equipment that holds a potent substance,
That would turn my eyes blood***shot*** red,

Feeding this craving with something, I was once fed,
From friends, who I found, wore a disguise,
You see they vividly told me how I'd feel in the sky,
But somehow left out how low I would dive,

It's hard to even lie, I thoroughly enjoyed it,
Felt like the only time that I was truly in air,
So now I'm playing tag with this deadly opponent,
Still chasing my first high, the mirage of despair,

Addicted, with that last ***shot*** pushing me over the edge,
And if that instant I was then dead,
My glassy eyes leaking tears, as I knelt and bowed my head,
What do you think The Lord would've said?

Or with revenge outlining my pupils,
I loaded a magazine, with lead,
To have the life flowing out of my infiltrator's body,
Like the beverage out of a keg,

I came up with the perfect plot,
An intricate scheme to get this person missin',
And the gun***shots*** I'mma give them,
Is of a different type of prescription,

I told them not to slip up,
Because playing with me is never just a game,
So I made sure they felt the brunt of my fury,
Anger was the gasoline fueling my internal flame,

Murderer, with that last ***shot*** pushing me over the edge,
And if that situation left me dead,
Stained with someone's blood on my skin, as I knelt
and bowed my head,
What do you think The Lord would've said?

BUT... what if I walked into a door,
In which all my goals had lead,
If off of one opportunity, I gained…
The once in a lifetime chance to put me ahead,

I had taken the time to prepare,
Staying on track like an unstoppable train,
Knowing that I would be ready and waiting,
Whenever that occasion came,

It then arrived, so that I could thrive,
And take that ***shot*** right into my dreams,
Building off of my failures, finding my purpose,
Not letting anything affect me that was considered obscene,

Determined, with that last ***shot*** pushing me over the edge,
And if, in my very moment, I dropped dead,
Having been able to see the Promised Land, before I knelt
and bowed my head,
Do you know what The Lord would've said?

He would say, "Well done, my son…
For running a good race and not being mislead,
Then I could follow Him to the thrown of grace,
And eternally break bread,

Every second, we live in a world,
Where our every choice will be accounted for,
And in the second you realize your time is up,
Would you be wishing that you still had more?

Tomorrow has never been promised,
And we've seen too many, in the wrong place, taken too fast,
So I say beware of the ***shots*** you take,
You never know, it just may be your last…

One Name

"There is a name…I love to hear"
That's sweeter to the ear, than anything's that's been said,
Has no need to ever be lead, as the follower of none,
Its position number is 1, atop the list of all names read,

Can raise the pronounced dead, to walk with the living yet again,
For this name holds something within, that conquers death, hell, and the grave,
It can take you to a resting place, in the stressful midst of a storm,
Keeping you comfortably warm, when the frigid winds of this life attack your base,

When it's used, you easily know the Adidas phrase, "Impossible Is Nothing,"
You're able to walk, no longer ducking, from the fiery darts of the enemy,
Not feeling your way through darkness timidly, this name outshines all of the lights,
The Lasik surgery of our physical sight, so that our path is no mystery,

In the stories passed down through history, it has been seen as the saving grace,
Like running to home plate, called safe, when empires could've called them out-then,
We saw how the devil wanted to re-route them, and this name kept them on track,
Refreshingly fulfilling in places of lack, as the ever-flowing fountain,

For it can place any massive mountain, into the depths of the abyss,
Upon no star-you need to wish, on this name you can rely,
To be the best of any ally, in every carnal and spiritual war,
What may have resembled a giant before, now looks like a giant bull's-eye,

It calms the tsunami tide of large oceans, comforts the stream of falling tears,
Being our solid rock for countless years, that we stand firm on and won't quiver,
For this name always delivers, faster than Jimmy Johns can attest to,
Even when speaking of fast food, there was manna,then water rushing out of a
rock like a river,

Because whether you think it, yell, or choose to whisper, you still can be saved,
Watch this hand-out-of-nowhere-raise, anyone from their sinking sand,
It needs no DNA but one Hope strand, a belief that lies in an open heart,
And with mustard seeds ordered A-La-Carte, what was labeled as can't is now can,

For this name belonged to a man, that's also a god, who is forever our king,
The one that took Satan's key ring, right after he hung and died for us,
But unlike dead things, he could never rust, he was still on a mission,
If you haven't heard it, please listen, that wonderful name is JESUS,

HIS name seems to be, no, is-what, I like to call above all names,
And if there's any doubt, he reigns, seated in heaven on the throne,
But not there alone, he also lives in me, seated at the alter of my temple,
And I'd like to tell you what he resembles since many have gotten this thing wrong,

HE's the man in the home, when a single mother thought she was by herself,
Hearing her cries as she knelt, assisting her when everyone else chose to judge,
HE's the hunger to go above and beyond, constantly encouraging you on the job,
Distracting your eyes from just staring at the clock, satisfied with giving just enough,

HE's the stillness whenever I'm stopped and cuffed, due to police racial profiling,
Though I'm thinking, "Yo, this dude is wildin," my actions won't reveal my thoughts,
So HE'll be the extra cells passed through my pulse, creating more tissue
to pad my cheek,
After these hits I receive, I can proceed turning to the other with no love lost,

HE's the courage not making me soft, supplying strength as the chief cornerstone,
Quickly sending all these others home, when infiltrators think they'll easily overcome,
Not backing down to anyone, but still trying to be peaceful at any rate,
So when bullies try to intimidate, I stand stiff with HIM, not running from,

He's the extra hydration in the burning sun, the additional oxygen that's passed
to my muscles,
Coming in ever-so subtle, when my limbs become weak so HE can brace,
And though I hear footsteps of those that chase, they never seem to measure up,
Despite the fact that my heart feels as if it will erupt, all I hear is HIM saying
"finish the race,"

HE's the murderer in our bodies; well let me rephrase, the complete painkiller,
The only healer of all our wounds, inflictions, diseases, viruses, and sickness,
Being able to answer the quickest, When doctors didn't even know how to approach
the issue,
But all the while in your patience, HE was with you,
To comfort and not just sit as a witness,

HE's the equation that the professor missed, helping me solve a frustrating problem,
While all else struggled, I could still blossom, on these tough test, quizzes, and final
exams,
Making me no longer cram, if I "C"-clear, in my bush a "Ram" always awaits,
So that my results are great, as long as I endure through my chance,

HE's the sustainer of my finance, when recession cause foreclosures and bankruptcy,
Filling the vacancy of income, when that word may have become past-tense,
Also acting as the invisible fence, surrounding my house when neighbors have
been attacked,
While those around me have walls that were cracked, HE made mine a little
more dense,

HE's the resistance to the undeniable force most of us know as peer pressure,
Not making me feel any lesser, when those seen as friends call me lame,
Instead my walk with HIM maintains, confident in who I am as a person,
Not letting their negative words worsen, but to a higher altitude I'll aim,

For HE's the one that lit the flame, so when my coolness isn't confirmed by the "in crowd,"
No doubt, because instead of being on fire in a pit, I'd rather be on fire for HIM,
And not dim, you see before Edison, He was the creator of another light-bulb business,
So in the sea of darkness, we would no longer take our gear to swim,

Carver may have revamped the farming system, but the lord was first to plant seeds in us,
So our growth is a must, and our harvest should always be the ripest on the leaf,
And even though Washington was voted first to lead, our God knew that position well,
That course HE had many years before sailed, as our true Commander and Chief,

Making it a no-brainer when I place my feet, into the footprints HE leaves behind,
Even if they are tracks that I must find, I believe that it is worth the search,
No matter how many think it's worst, serving a god that you can't visually see,
I like how my imaginative faith won't limit me, because HE's not confined to this Earth,

And HE, knowing HIS own worth, thought enough to give HIS life for us,
So I must say the name JESUS, for I will forever follow Yahweh,
Oh, and that's not to be confused with me following Ya'll Way, please understand,
We all truly have a hand, in whether we want to rise above a life of waste,

To become the image-sinners see of Christ's face, though they don't see HIM with natural eyes,
But it fascinates me how HE shows HIMSELF, in everything that HE provides yet the same,
HE was the spotless lamb slain, the messiah, and though in Espanol he's called Jesùs,
HE is Emmanuel, the Resurrection, Life, and Truth, all falling under…One Name…

...All true Christians know it best…and spell it J..E..S..U..S!...

Pure Essence

From the depths of Africa you arose,
Silky-smooth skin, lips as petaled rose,
Mastered, made perfectly,
Like when the maker created you-time froze,

To put other obligations on hold,
And outline you after no mold,
To place a twinkle in your eye-
That could never shine from pure gold,

And the stars become jealous,
When they see your beauty unfold,
Just because of your natural glow,
And your mere presence is universal,

Your voice is as smooth as fine wine-
In a crystal goblet,
And words are renowned,
Even when pronounced as silent as droplets,

Persuasive manner turns "not-lets"-
Into a single answer "yes,"
Leaving your victims only to wonder-
Of this power you possess,

This fantastic black magic,
Residing in the deepest of chocolate,
Mysterious as a diary confession-
Encaged in a keyless locket,

Nonetheless enticing as dessert delicacies,
Sweet as the cherry that sits atop it,
And a taste alone-makes man lose control,
Like the pilot of a malfunctioning cockpit,

Walk with a stride-magnetized,
To attract the opposite sex's eyes,
With just a glace of thick thighs,
Men have become paralyzed,

To see this everyday wonder walk by,
Calm as a lake on a fall day,
And a cool breeze makes her fly,
Like graceful butterflies in May,

Few are able to watch her sleep,
Like a new winter coat of fresh snow-she lays,
And ones that have stolen a peek,
Sees her uniqueness like every snow flake,

Her character is great,
With internal strength to make opposition buckle,
Her majestic poise can intimidate,
Without curved bulging muscles,

Which men bow to one knee-
To explain their love for you,
To commit their life-
Because your aura is essential,

Your ability to make a man's ego feel equal,
Whether in a motel room or a suite that's presidential,
To gain your respect doesn't come easy,
But its effects are monumental,

Because you've come from plantations & minorities,
To having your own independence,
But can still complete a man,
Like a period that stands next to a sentence,

So virtuous & phenomenal-
Has to come with a black woman's presence,
Modern day Nubian queens-
With nothing but-pure essence...

Rock It Legit

They were yelling crucify him, now-days we just throw on a crucifix,
Don't recognize the story, no symbolism for your swanging necklace,
So we flood the cross with diamonds, blang out the Jesus piece,
By the chain we identify him, with little regard for his legacy,

Always upgrading stones so the new is better than the predecessor,
Round and princess-cut, flawless owned, the quality can be of no lesser,
To sport then throw in a dresser at home, when we're out it's always on,
To impress while we roam, the lifestyle matching the charm
we've seemed to postpone,

Wondering to myself the effects had HE put HIS purpose on hold,
To step down off the steeple, and impress the on-looking people,
Those terms put together would've equaled the worst equation for
our lives,
But we won't share this light, use the ice because it stays so bright,

Then snatch, jack, rob, and fight because we don't have it like that,
And if we do, it's just a signal to dude, that he isn't as hard as he act,
So for some clear one's, we'll have paramedics show up first on the scene,
Yet no ambulance sirens scream when Jesus was that diamond in
the rough for me,

*Yet no ambulance sirens scream when Jesus was that diamond in the
rough for me*

That changes my definition of a real blood diamond,
The blood, sweat, and tears spent so now we all could be shining,
The death of someone containing no indentation, who watched
our creation,
To feel the sensation, that there's little appreciation for his emancipation
visitation,

The proclamation of this life-changing information-
That we could share to those staring at the rocks,
But to few, these jewels sitting in the mold, hold weight, so the
example stays blocked,
Do all our dirt while these chains and ropes swing like pendulums,
Our conscience has faded, no indigestion, we've taken life's tums,

Some crosses sitting on the chest and stomachs of those hungry to do evil,
And still they think they'll fly toward the heaven like seagulls,
Yet they land on the water, till it dries and brings drought,
Their crosses turning on angles, leaving their hearts X'd out,

Held up by a guy that caught you slipping and then ran ya piece,
And ironically Jesus was placed on a cross between two thieves,
This momentous should carry more weight than just the frozen additions,
Pitiful how you can rock his logo around your neck without any religion,

Am I the only one that has evidence for what the crucifix should really represent?
That it's much more than a justification for wealth without the proper reverence,
I just want to persuade more people to wear this precious item legit,
And stop creating more examples of acceptable hypocrites,

For we should not only wear the cross, it's also something-we should carry,
Continuing HIS legendary story, not letting it end at where HE was buried,
For some see that symbol as nothing more than a day that one man died,
But I see it as a struggle he endured so in my heart he could reside…

That's why, even if not physically, on my chest, this charm forever lies…

Priceless or Priced-More

How high is the price of life, is this an answerless question?
If so, why does it take a little bread to turn one's direction?
Or a little lead to the head to destroy this tag-less perfection,
And to create with little spray that spreads, after internal injection,
.....That was in the end a result of an internal affair in-correction......

Disregard for the numbers behind the dollar sign that go towards infinity,
May have been the virus entering the community,
That infected you-him-her-and me,
As the delicacy of life is ignored, the more it becomes clearance,
The overlooked rack in the store-then to the finer couture,
So easily do we leave theses on-sale lives on the floor,

Bonjour, is what we trying to say, to get money, no matter if lives pass away,
I guess since these would-be antiques are easily made,
Lacking respect created this trade; holocaust, reservations, and
imported slaves,
Even the young lives of soldiers we lay in patriotic graves,
Because the kings in the white house move pawns like a chess game,

A-shame, how we buy who we want to flaunt a certain name,
And lames we pay no attention to so they gain none of our change,
Our change-the switch of persona when we feel one is worth more,
When we're all equally priceless, some in the front window,
other's in back of the store,
Some in high commodity, fragile sand-tile pottery,
Others demanded only when there's no foreseen comradery,

So the image of love or boredom leads us to play with each other's biology,
Pushing each others buttons like engineers testing technology,
So how much is him or her, when they lay with he or she?
Causing a seed to leave, teleporting babies or STDs,
Did you ever see daddy leave, gone with the wind through forest trees,
And you now hear the echo of the cash register, "cha-ching",

And the child or disease grows, ignoring each one or both,
Then on with life we go, grab some champagne and toast,
The price we pay for life today, most care-less to ever know,
So we create and then take, life-tags with prices on we debate,
Because we add 2 cents to what we thought you weren't worth anyway,

Then skate, when we should recognize we all could be great,
People's spirit, soul, and mind, priced that the richest couldn't make,
As they fly at high altitudes, swinging moods that make bad attitudes,
Cause their appreciation to depreciate like that thing on 24" shoes,
But the price of humanity comes as vanity, seemingly a common insanity,

So the baby that lies in the crib, on itself pees,
With no cleaning lady, because she's mad at daddy,
As the young one on the street runs franticly free,
Neglected-because in him, no one believes,
The young adult thrown to college or the harshness of war,
Never pushed hard enough to soar, since no one's trying to help anymore,

The adult that takes no more chances,
Sits in the position they were handed with no future glances,
And the elderlies patiently waiting to eventually push up daises,
Because the price of life was never printed on mainstream,
Or given the same critique as that shiny diamond gleam,

So we'll just creep slow when our allowance runs low,
Just to cash you in, to re-up our cash flow,
Sad the things we don't know, and what we don't value, we abuse,
Not stopping, they'll continue to put their price higher than you,

Until then we'll never be opposite of the sign equal,
And the price of life will diminish and diffuse,
But how high is the price of life? The question I'll still pose to you,
Because to me, priceless is an understatement, but your value, you choose....

No Shelter

Cold sidewalks, and cold shoulders
Turned on low-lives, with heads lowered
Not a-loan in sight, leave them alone; that's different
Not wanting their type coming around like rotor's.

Like addicted smokers; standing outside in all weather
But this group stands here having no place better
...to go...like food uneaten in restaurant-like conditions
Good rest-you-want, but that order's seen rarely ever.

There's no a la carte, their shopping cart now replaces
Fancy place-settings at well-known expensive places
Where uptight faces, would judge by appearance alone
Knowing nothing about how the mind races...

In a life of helter skelter, when having no shelter
Where no matter the forecast, they often still swelter...
Under these heavy pressures; of a world, often, so cold
An oxymoron; and "I-see-moron" is what some say about failure.

When truthfully, but by grace...there go I
She could be that gal, and I-that guy
Dare we look down on someone in unfavorable conditions
As if we are just that much more sky-high,

Even now-seasoned christians, were first taken in rags
Into a perfect place, undeserved, changing our sad state to glad
A thankful state for more than just these material possessions
But more-so for the one who supplies all that we have.

For allowing us to be children of a Father with no reassurance
from Maury,
For the talents that each of us were given, being used for HIS glory,
For a place to lay our head in peace, when all was lost,
And for not letting our low points be the end of our story,

The great news is God still calls a line reaching our land.
On the receiving side HE waits patienty with outstretched hands
And if we'd understand and just transmit, openly, our hearts
He would gladly fulfill, exceeding our every demand,

Making it mandatory that we assist those in need
So others can partake of the fruit harvested by our seeds
Life is empty with no legacy, we should yearn to share
Finding joy in the furtherance of others, and not in our greed,

So give thanks in all things, no matter the surroundings
Whether in a mansion or homeless, in a sea of life drowning
Whether on top of a hill, or in the lowest point of a valley
Keep your thoughts positive until the day of your crowning.

Where your heart is, there is, also-inevitably, your home
And when we find treasures in more places than the
things that we own
Life then resembles a higher calling, not of this world
As children of a king, finding comfort, at his throne.

Kill-Joy Manufacturing

She was there when the blueprint was laid,
Though there are many downfalls that lie array-she pursues
Author, creator and producer of this product made,
And to manufacture-it was a large sum paid,

Whether it be her dignity, integrity, or virginity,
It seemingly depreciated almost instantly,
Sending her to open a locked room,
Which she did only using a supplier's key,

And production began-
As the operator gained her approval,
Only forward motion on this "line"-
No impermissible removal,

Speeding like a foreign convertible 2-door,
But cruising like a smooth sedan,
Though what's in production,
Would probably sit in the car-seat of a van,

Or hold someone's hand-when crossing the street,
Because this item she constructed-contains a heartbeat,
Her machinery creates an entity full of life,
But the schedule of delivery came to her as a surprise,

Which she must now keep a secret,
To still be looked at as decent,
Otherwise widen eyes would look at her like she'd committed treason
Because she brought out this product in the wrong season,

So she turns to deletion-
The option of scraping this unwanted item,
To separate her-self from it,
Like a busted tire from a dented rim,

Like a immigrant factory worker-
That she chose to deport,
She decides to cut all ties,
And unplug the life support,

Otherwise known as abort,
That's what it's called in this plant,
Seeds buried inside that she'd like to return,
But, sadly, she can't,

Sweat-shop love making after hours-
Reconstructed into reproduction,
And fear mixed with irresponsibility
Couldn't take the repercussions,

So sudden the object comes-naturally,
Automated-no need for a battery,
And instead of being elated,
Chose to toss what was fabricated,

This life with new beginnings,
Is forced shortly to meet its end,
Didn't ask to be made,
And still after, ignores its opinion,

Made to be placed in a trash can,
Presence taken as a grain of sand,
Just to be able to experience-
A trimester lifespan,

Neglecting the size;
It nonetheless is still alive,
Awaiting the chance to live
A newly presented fulfilling life,

To be the next engineer, doctor,
Entertainer, or lead to teach,
Preacher, lawyer, or accountant,
Even our commander and chief,

But wasn't even allowed to speak,
Or able to touch, hear, feel, or see,
Simply because the plant manager-felt-
That she wasn't ready,

The plan fine-printed the outcome,
So from the new age product she runs,
Though it was presented as a downfall,
On the presentation page #1,

When looked at as negative,
It should really be viewed as a blessing,
To bring life in this world,
Though it caused her to start stressing

So her factory shuts-down,
Emptiness inside like recession lay-offs,
Until this plant manager finds-
Another partnering boss,

Another operator to work her line,
Helping to manufacture invaluable goods,
If a surprise should happen again,
Repeat her reaction-she would,

Killing one after another,
Results repeat in succession,
Eventually shutting her machinery down,
Mill closed from internal depression,

Never truly understood the lesson taught,
Not innocent of murder-despite what was thought,
Just was throwing away incomplete products,
Never used a gun to get them shot,

And after the first-she was left vacant,
Tried to refill with plant working replacements,
A multiple story-high building,
That would never allow her out of the basement,

Because embarrassment, pressure, or conviction,
Sent her morals to retortion,
To resort to the option-
Of considering abortion,

A plant only kept up and running-
To produce then destroy,
The joyous life of an infant,
Better known as a kill-joy...

Clocked

Seconds, minutes, hours; Days, weeks, months, years;
Decades, centuries, millenniums, all containing one from of measurement shared,
Time; The one thing everyone can say that they have,
Though unable to grab, it's available to grasp,
Just line up your task and see how it works in your favor,
And time will unwind the scroll that reads off the results of your labor,

The value of time is uncompared to anything else,
Can bring wealth or poverty, depends on if it's used properly,
So is time literally money? Or is money time's priority?
Which one has the authority? Either way I say grind accordingly,

Look in each other's eyes adoringly,
But if you waste my time, do you really love me?
Did you ever take the time to think…nah, so I was left waiting to be better treat,
Then time slowly revealed to me, that no better treatment was in your pharmacy,

Now weeks, months, and years, spent on someone,
And left hanging like in a jungle gym, though I am a gem,
My mine of quality time was never opened,
Left hoping time will be better spent, then on to the next person,

Our lives consist of it, without it we're nothing,
Just as those that lay in the coffins, grave hand-cuffing,
But the tick-tock on the walls, wrist, phones, computers, and ovens,
Is easily passed unused, when you not on the rise like muffins,

Because past millennium's information wasn't interesting,
Ignored century's histories, since that ancestry didn't seem to relate to me,
Wasted decades of life, which lead to death, stressed buy unnecessary strife,
Years passing with your families tears,
Dying after months in the hospital, when their hopes turned to fears,

Starting with weeks of you in Acoma,
Body traumatized after days of the doctor working on ya,
Because it took the ambulance hours to come,
After minutes passed by on the phone with an operator from 911,
All stemmed from the second that bullet entered your body, from out of that gun,

So you can't tell me the object of time isn't a valuable one,
Even the lord needed time to create the earth, moon, and the sun,
So do you find yours constructively missing?
Is it filled with orders from persons, places, and things?

Or do you have so much it is hard for you not to do anything,
Wasting away until someone picks you up, like the trash on
collection morning,
It instead, you should be adorning-so when your end comes,
You'll be able to say confidently that you time spent was well done.......

A Loyal Charade

I believed that long-awaited, special one, was you,
You were the fountain- I threw my coins into,
And made a wish, ever-so-fully bliss,
That to me, you'd committed-ly, be true,

Different than the stereotypical image,
So I place you in my top 1 percentage,
Since you appeared to be faithful, I in-turn was grateful,
And my time spent with you was considered a privilege,

Freeing the inner me, having the chance to be real,
Showing you myself raw, without the outer seal,
My love with no expiration date, so you could always partake,
And you ate-feeding off my heart's mouth-watering meal,

With this refrigerated relationship-so chill-I often ignored,
The stomach growl of your inner emotions that seemed to want more,
More of a different entre, more-like the soup of the day,
So you swayed-as if you no longer liked what I had in store,

Acting in the moment-without taking time to contemplate,
Jeopardizing our future, because you couldn't use your "brakes,"
Causing a "collision" of two anatomies, this "accident" that
        brings-me-agony,
You being "hit" with the tempting entice of another's warm embrace,

Bringing me back this "body-shop-touched-up" figure I thought I knew,
Your love had been refurbished, which no longer felt new,
Fragments of you re-aligned, your "out-of-sight" actions-now
        "in-my-mind",
So our chemistry fades like particle erosion in test tubes,

And since our relationship was the dependent variable,
Its strength weakens when our foundation splits like speakers in stereo,
This foundation built from trust, you broke up-alluding to lust,
When you let a 3rd party-share your exclusive material,

When discovered, I found you played the part, like charades,
Role-playing, when I just naturally wanted you to be what you portrayed,
Committed to me-loyally, instead of you screwing me-royally,
Planting a seed deep in me that only internally breeds hate,

Then externally I want to bring you the same pain that I feel,
But not to you only, also to your partner that aided in the kill-
And the slaughter of my inner emotions, who spilled all my love potion,
That could easily heal my wounded heart from being ill,

And no matter what I do, it never seems to be enough,
I feel so used, like a vehicle-sitting in a lot-for sale-with rust,
Taking my love for a ride, then placing it to the side,
When he-busted in-her, like I did the windows on your Lexus

And when that flow was ejected, so followed your respect for me,
Don't get me twisted; every single step was wrong that lead
you to the peak,
From your lustful imagination, to your cooperative participation,
Since you made or let it happen,
You probably don't think I'm important enough to keep,

But I know my worth, and can love myself in spite of your actions,
Even though my mind keeps slipping, with time, I'll steadily gain
traction,
This pain won't always constrain, and soon-from thinking of you-
I'll restrain,
Because I'll never depend on anyone for my soul's satisfaction,

And I regret that I retaliated, it was the human in me,
Because, like you I succumbed to my situation, though it was caused
by misery,
These two wrongs didn't make a right, proven by my drenched pillow
at night,
But my dreams reveal a better future, which comforts me while I sleep,

The things people don't respect they will eventually come to lose,
Thinking a person's love will wait,
No matter what you do, like an alarm set on snooze,
A scarred heart is hard to heal; it plays back old memories like movie reels,
And until you can forgive and forget you'll constantly wear this love bruise …

Substitution

The motto is "finance before romance", for a slow dance with the underground,
So unbuckle your pants, as she stands, watching you slowly take them down,
Showing her-her paycheck, not what's revealed, but that's the image she gets,
Her private parts for your money, a trade not perfect, but nonetheless worth it,

Because she expects to be paid, money's her compensation, your's? To get laid,
Hiding the fact she's afraid, each time she walks that dark stairway,
Behind door #1, her legs divorce, once again separate...
Working hard to please her supervisor in all the right ways,

You punch her clock in and out on a tight schedule, with no time to waste,
And don't address the title overtime with a nonnegotiable raise,
You see the cash is the leash that ties her cat to the gate,
So you can ask but won't receive until she's confident the money's straight,

Ironically her nightly income is more than some make in a full day,
So the drop-out has a hustle providing much more than minimum wage,
Started at the minimal age, because older men wanted to play,
Which ultimately lead her astray from the correct pathway,

And getting high takes your mind off yours and other's lives you've ruined,
Yet they're still pursuing, and the trade once again transmits,
No kissing & no romancing, that's how she's stays mysterious,
On her heart, no man, again, will ever see the sign entrance,

She tells him to sit, then lay back and enjoy till the job is finished,
Don't love him, just here to please him, till it comes time to leave him,
A lot of experience under her belt, so you might say that she's seasoned,
Internal treason, but she keeps calling these tricks the traitor,
Life no longer knows any reason, so used to removing all her layers,

Everyone loves her for her favors, and the things that she'll do,
Pimps love collecting her money, customers love tasting her fruit,
Leaving their icing on top, then on the dresser leaving the loot,
So everyday feels like her birthday, getting cake, while staying in that suit,

But hoping that she'll survive and not get blown out like the candles,
Because trying to assume a trick is legit, is too much for her mind to handle,
Closed minded, you'll never find her open like toes in beach sandals,
So nightly, she stuffs her stockings with something new, like fireplace mantles,

It's a rotten life to live, to get something, but more value is what you give,
But her view of her body from past casualties made her unreceptive,
And she couldn't heal old wounds, with her lack of antiseptic,
So prostitution was her substitution for no positive objective....

On a day-to-day basis, we see traces of black on black crime,
Also the effect of things done in the dark that ironically make it to prime-time,
Our articles are used to collect re-appearing filth, like a pipe holding sink grime,
It seems we see many just going through the motions, like a large group of mimes,

In this world, often-times- pitch-black, is all someone can see,
As a spectator on-looking the American Negro Baseball League,
A dark pitch, a dull tune, so many potential notes off key,
As darkness surrounds, blinding the ability to read a classic harmonious "peace",

There are shadows where evil tendencies lurk,
Where things that are unknown try to hurt,
For when things are not seen, they in-turn see you-
Being in harm's way, as a susceptible perk,

As an opportunity to play on the fears that you quietly cover,
Using tactics to obscure your view, a wide-screen vision that's smothered,
Exhausting your hopes and dreams for the future, as fumes-let out by a muffler,
So that we'll join in-on the misery that causes others to continually suffer,

A state that is destitute of necessary wisdom and knowledge,
Of a dull quality that has not ever been polished,
Like an account shown with previous financial blockage,
The remains are of no significant deposit,

Dismal...when really we should be more instrumental,
The backbone of all things good, and the structure of a walking temple,
Having the ability to look back on problems as something that's now considered simple,
While striving for righteousness and straying away from being sinful,

Not letting ourselves be influenced by the norm, of the unenlightened,
But being the moonlight at midnight, the reason dark places are brightened,
Not giving up in the midst of a fight, instead battling like a titan,
Looking any challenge in the face-not easily wavered or frightened,

So with courage we venture into the light, set apart-with pride,
Walking thru the valley of the shadow of death, we fear no evil that arrives,
Having someone much greater operating as our internal driving guide,
So when on-lookers see our success they see also what lives inside,

For its been said that our eyes are the windows of the soul,
But our fruits stem from the branches of the vine, from which we grow,
The vine of the most high, rooted from above by a heavenly host,
But we'll never brag about what we have nor selfishly depend on what
we gross,

The exposure we then share is hard to be undone,
For when we've come into our full being we'll begin to shine like the sun,
No longer having to "light-into" someone if they pick on us for fun,
Instead we'll put light-into the ones who want to be what we've become…

"Light-headed" the point when imagination begins to radiate,
And "light-hearted" with peace because we're preserved by marvelous grace,
Under a bushel, you'll never see the flame of our candle-stick placed,
Because we're confident in our talents creating a legacy that can't be erased...

By stepping into the light-as the example of what's right,
In a world where darkness is prevalent and mediocre is the popular type,
Everyday someone's looking upon a star to wish they may, and wish
they might,
But I wish they'll chose a star like us to use as a role-model for their life,

To glorify the true and living god of all heaven and earth,
For HE is the one that made us to be these shining beacons from birth,
Whether or not we choose to be is either our blessing or curse,
But when we choose the brighter-side of living, we acknowledge our
undeniable worth...

Who Told You?

Who told you, you couldn't cut it?
I mean, did they own all the cutlery,
That you could've used-to remove,
These lines, they hang over your head like a puppet,

That you should remain less than average,
As they savagely beat up on your ideas-
And opinions, like they hold less weight,
So through life you'd carry on, as jet-liner baggage,

Who told you, you couldn't do it?
Like they took the time to exclude-
Your name, from every single NIKE commercial,
And made sure your Gatorade bottle was completely diluted,

So when you're asked the question – "Is it in you?"
You'd doubt yourself every time..."Like umm...
Maybe...well, I really don't know"
Like your heart is a smoke screen you can't see into,

Who told you, you didn't matter?
Did they meet with every single chemist to agree-
You're the only living specimen, without substance,
Seeing you as anti-matter, when you ask, "cant-i-matter?"

Like you were created as the element in elementary,
Becoming intrinsic with the word "simplistic,"
So your more like non-existent, and your net worth-
Shouldn't be discovered on accident, like serendipity,

Who told you, you were a loser?
Did they reformat the word succeed, to imply-
That your seed-sucks, by inheriting sub standard-
Efforts that come up short on every ruler,

Like all the Referees were hired to place you last,
And like every stripe that's on their shirt,
Your results would be just that black and white,
Color-blind to the view of having flying colors as you pass,

Who told you, you were stupid?
Did they program your central nervous system-
To input, everything that your senses receive-
In a way that appears more convoluted,

So your thought process would be a mess,
Making everything you utter, sound like clutter,
A grammar hard to distinguish, so people ask, "is that English?"
This language barrier, just adding to your mental stress,

Who told you, you had low self esteem?
Like they stole the coals you could've applied-
To your fire inside, that burning desire,
To become exactly who you always dreamed,

Since heat was made to rise, and yours remains low,
There is not enough internally, to raise your head,
And we always take the path we envision-
So staring at the ground keeps your life downward spiraled,

Who told you, that you were ugly?
Did they connect themselves to every mirror-
You'd look into, so you'd see yourself only through their eyes,
Viewing your image a lot more roughly,

Like your face contains no special attraction,
Your feature's presentation, won't be-
Sold out or premier, since masses don't appeal,
On your genes came the label "dissatisfaction,"

Who told you, that you were weak?
Like they nicknamed you after "7 days",
Because during that time they stunted your growth,
So your muscles wouldn't show throughout your physique,

Making courage something you could never attain,
So you'd be discouraged to fight through all barricades,
Show your face to your fears, and strive through grievous tears,
Since 'motionless' is "comfortable," that's how you'd remain,

Who told you their race was better than yours?
Did they stand at the finish line-of time, with a-
Stopwatch to see which of our colors passed first,
So they assume they could manage while you do their chores,

Like they're more of a person because of their pigmentation,
With more than 2 hands, 2 feet, more than 5 fingers and toes-
On each, their brains on full while yours on E,
So every time they speak, they'd rock your foundation,

Well...Who told them, they were an expert on you?
Like they took a class on your Make-up,
Culture, Knowledge, and your Appearance, and to pass-
They'd list all the limitations-that you'd agreed to,

How many people have we given control?
Not knowing our own capability, so we-
Hand over the remote, for them to play these-
Costly mind-games like a your a game console,

Yet there was no consolation prize in sight,
Just more lonely nights, the feeling of not being loved,
Heart-broken, beaten, and down trodden,
Like nothing in this world is ever right,

And when you're alone, somehow you still hear-
In repetition, the things that "they" had told you,
What the ears continue to take in, the mind will replay,
So after all their direction, you're now able to steer,

The point-where you take over-telling yourself,
What you can't do or be, when instead-
you can repeat the words, From the one who knows-
all about you, undoubtedly the best,

HE told you, you were fearfully and wonderfully made,
Like HE created you in his image,
And through HIM all things can be finished,
Fighting the good fight as long as you carry along faith,

HE told you the race wasn't given to the swift,
Nor the battle to the one that's strong,
But as long as you endure to the end,
Onto your 1st place pedestal you would lift,

HE told you if you'd ask, seek, and knock,
The windows of Heaven would then open-
Fulfilling all off your needs and wants,
Without having any items out of stock,

HE told you HE would be with you,
When you walk through the valley of the shadow-
Of death, not fearing any evil,
Somehow remaining ever-so blissful,

HE told you that goodness and mercies,
Would follow you all the days of your life,
And one day we could reach the destination-
If we hold fast to what we've foreseen,

So don't continually listen to a person,
Not having your best intention in mind,
Allowing them to persuade you negatively,
Causing you to overall worsen,

There is someone speaking if you listen,
And if you ask why you should consider-
Anything that HE has to say, it's because-
HE created us all as we should be, without anything missing…

The Game Room

Find a seat in this place,
There's many spots for you to sit,
I call it the game room,
And the same I tend to spit,

Like I'm shining your emotions,
With words containing a twist,
Intoxicatingly pulling you in,
Off the sweet flavoring you get,

Its somewhat magical, yet tactical,
How this game table stands,
Rarely factual, so my fables,
Keep you in a fantasy land,

Or candy land, with this candy man,
Sticking strictly to my plan,
To heat you up in ways,
Gas never heated a frying pan,

My one and only, well at least today,
In fact you're helping me expand,
Serving as the 3rd queen,
Setting up a "full house" in my poker hand,

And my poker face mask you from my true colors
Like a box of crayons,
So in a hand of poke-her,
I lose less in this game of chance,

On this word romance, don't be surprised-
To find me rolling a die,
To pick the number of the one,
I'll be romancing tonight,

Though it's rarely by candlelight,
The spark we make-keeps a dyed room bright,
And while my view is picturing you,
My closed caption may be reading hindsight,

Because I keep a few options,
With enough baby-girls for adoption,
And when I deliver them in my room,
I service their needs like John Hopkins,

Then skip, so I pretty much hop-scotch them,
And soon I'll be back,
The next time I'm in the mood-
To run a full night of tag,

And do I compare them….well yea,
But I'm not really one to brag,
C'mon, I mean it's all in the game,
So you know I gotta keep stats,

Since I scrabble facts, and mix channels,
Like I'm shuffling multiple tracks,
I can play anything they wanna hear,
Exactly when they needed that,

When I want to play spades,
They store enough, and then won't extract,
Because I need them birth controlled,
I only like working with spaded cats,

And every answer is exact,
Telling them "I'm not ready to start a family just yet,"
Seeing that my response is in tact,
I find they aren't too taken a-back,

Like Mattel, mostly what I "tell" them,
Eventually leads to a "Mat",
Seeing them when it works for me,
So just wait till I initiate contact,

Its like an imaginary contract,
And my sheets contain obvious proof,
And since I obviously clean those,
Each time this contract is renewed,

So I free-agent myself,
Making me openly able to move,
Not fully committing, or really attaching,
So I play this way the entire season through,

With my 2 truths and 1 lie,
I play on their naive mental youth,
Playing Uno, or what I call You-Know,
To see what they really knew,

I find just like Parker Brothers,
They really don't have a clue,
On how to really Park-A-Brutha,
So this lack of info I abuse,

Letting them all get their turn,
Like I set up my own kissing booth,
And the form of payment I took,
Leaves them feeling violated and confused,

Later finding I'm not at all sorry,
Like the board game their accustomed to,
I have no shame in the things I did,
And the one's I'll continue to do,

I gave them the feelings that they needed,
And the ones they wanted and never knew,
And maybe I exaggerated the whole phrase,
That "1 head wasn't better than 2,"

....

But whoa whoa, wait, I'm getting ahead of myself,
See cuz baby, this is just about you and me...
You gotta body that'll change a nigga,
And I see the dime my life needs,

Girl, it was a hole in my puzzle,
And you're shaped like the missing piece,
If I was to leave here with out you,
My heart would internally bleed....

Like Sunday morning, you could get me with ease,
And most def. get it....believe,
So let's remove ourselves from this spot,
Like I wanna do your satin 2-piece...

(And what do you think she said?)....
Well her answer kinda confused me actually,
It was a little different from the norm,
Her response was "What about me?"

And I'm looking around like...
"Honey! I been talking bout only you!
I'm sayin I need that long lasting flavor,
And you got that juicy fruit I wanna chew,"

She says, "Yea I've heard all about my body,
And the things you wanna do,
But while I'm giving you sides of me,
What substance can you offer off your menu,"

Umm....wow.....and I guess my off-cued silence,
Induced her to politely say no,
I don't know, I'm not used to-
Bringing too much else to the table,

And I'm somewhat out my comfort zone,
I've felt my share of rejection befo(re),
But it was something about the way-
This one did it to me though,

I've neva been one to get them all,
But 9 out of 10, are cut from the same mold,
Most of them would be ready-
To jump on my stick like pogo,

Let me hit them and run,
Then off on my horse like polo,
But she rolled out pulling a different number,
And surprised me like bingo,

And this slight tingle I feel,
Can't be remorse, yea right…
I'm used to all this,
I've been the joker on countless dark nights,

But this feeling is insight,
Noticing I'm a felon of a different type,
Cuz I'm just a spin on a con-way's path,
Playing these girls in the Game of Life…

Wait-Loss

My heart sunk when I heard the news
Did I really just lose
The one I had only pictured myself with
But left in dark rooms?

Still gracing the scenes that I dreamt
I never knew what that meant
I figured time would reveal its truth
So on with life, I went.

Splitting since, I had these goals to pursue
Sadly, none, were entitled you
The outcome made me think we'd still work out
Since you stood alone in my rear-view,

As a previous destination for later dates
I could run home to; "safe"
Since you were secure, solid, and impregnable
What I "preyed" for, but never chased.

Now I can't cultivate my intake
Because they're all second rate
Playing with this food, not fully attentive
They're not made of what you "concentrate…"

…On…

Knowing why they won't hold me forever
Mainly because I've had better
I'll basically lick, stick, then let go
"Fe-mail-handling"; Girls as letters.

When really I hate it, cus' I'm not a dog
Just got caught in the fog
Where girls don't demand you be an open book
But settle for your prologue.

Indispensable's something they don't know
So they settle for optional
Becoming easy to get, like sterling silver
Instead of that polished gold;

The color of honey tasted in Promised Land
In this wilderness; I can't stand
To that, I'm a lame, cus' it's just not my lane
Easiness bores a hard-working man.

But I can't totally blame them either
As a man, you just look weaker
Teasing these girls, doing things made for lovers
Simply because they charge cheaper.

Like "I have needs," is a valid excuse
Really, all I needed…was you
But I couldn't straight up tell you that
My pride swallowed that truth.

Now I long for the days of a challenge
When women kept you in balance
Feeling the strength of her at your side
To go at anything…valiant.

So, for you, I find myself wishin'
See…you caused me to listen…
As I broke down your advance thought process
Like encrypted inscriptions.

Your panoramic views were so wide
…Instead of your thighs
I silently enjoyed knowing you were unique
With power sitting behind your eyes,

A grounded foundation set below your heels,
And a drive, pushing your "will"
These others keep throwing me for a loop
While you're the perfect catch on any field.

But I guess, he caught on to that too
And I wonder, how he'll do?
Will he value what he has, fulfill your dreams,
Blessing you, like after "achoo!"?

Or will he release you like the sneeze I did
Then try and cover it, like a wig,
Will you lay your cards all out on the table,
And find he's prone to renege?

Either way it's no longer my issue
My "wait-loss"; of a love so true
I struggle in search of another that real
Feeling like Mary J., in 92'.

So I title you, "one that got away"
My heart's an inferno, like Dante's
You were the catch I fumbled under pressure
Not fighting for you to the end of play.

How many good people did we leave,
Or watch helplessly, as they proceed
As egos, disagreements, angers, and frustrating moments,
Seemed to out-weigh future lb.'s.

Still running the good scenes through our memories
Like our favorite DVD's
Playing alternate endings in the place of what happened
Since the real version doesn't please.

Mentally recollecting these shredded scraps
To rebuild this collapse
This building didn't have to be left up in air
Had we shared all, like wire-taps.

So I say to all who will listen
Respect the person you're given
Love can, most times, be a funny thing
Not so, when it's missin'.

If you have that "one," hold them forever
Fight through all types of weather
With a positive outlook, you're bound to realize
All things eventually get better.

That's who you'd rather be in tribulations with
Not someone willing to leave you, swift
At times when everything might look down
You need that one, made to upshift.

You only get one shot at this life
And I too, just hope I aim right
Because "True Love", like any great opportunity
Doesn't always come around twice.

White Pearl

Come into my harsh environment, and get you some of these white pearls,
That fresh vanilla coloring, but we not talking ice cream swirls,
Get them; spread them all over the table, Package up and throw on some labels,
Pearls caught up in underground transactions, getting customers wired like cable,

Addicted, creeping-through picking up quickly, to diversely wear them internally,
This underground railroad they on, supports a different type of economy,
These pearls usually held under lock & key, sitting out rottenly, but wrapped up nicely,
So their fresh for the next shopper, trying to re-up on the nightly,

To practician insufflations on this single line formation.....These pearls are chewed, smoked, melted down, and injected to have the same ending relation,
The high, the flyness of the pearl's natural external shiny layer,
Wearing these pearls in ya system, got you feelin electric like a taser,
They bring extra adrenaline when you've been hypnotized then mesmerized,

The feeling of an on-air glide, when saltwater pearls redden glassy eyes,
Tantalizing depressions arise without this prized possession in hand,
So dudes crack heads to get pearls outta you, instead of cracking white oysters and clams,

White oysters are the white lawyers defending Columbian, Mexican & Brazilian clams,
So in this arena, we Americans, can just be considered as the hardcore fans,
We buy the tickets, set-up "will-calls," Ticket-scalp, but don't control the game-plan,
We can just supply our supporters the opportunity to watch the pearl-movement game from the stands,

As these pearls stay guarded by all types of protection,
Semi-auto, AK's, and Sawed Off's with aim perfection,
G's hoping 5-0 doesn't have the nerve to arrest them,
Undress them-then dress them in that unattractive suit,

Either way with no delay, they can still get that weight to you,
Make that 800-Call-Collect move, 'Heard dude want a pearl round and small"
At the same time-you give my nigga the money-My man's hands you the "eight-ball,"
Still got his jewelry-shop making special pearl deliveries,

Can keep the units trafficking without his immediate presence to oversee,
So with his new cubicle with bars, the boss never slows corporate moves,
Even though he's caught up in the system with no tie on this suit,

It's a profession with the arrows pointing in the negative direction,
Lives lack correction needed when these pearls are in one's possession,
Even fills the cavities of the prostitutes and the hoes,
Sweating-going through security, to reach the other side of the globe,
While the hometown traffickers stuff their cars with these O's,

Because in the dark corners of the city, this is all that they know,
...and value, not anything on the level of what's taught in college classrooms,
Though teachers taught them too, to protect these ovular jewels,
Their test weren't in desk-but wearing vest while they shoot,

Though no director yells cut, so you better pass the jewelry inspection,
if you get dropped-good luck, if you get caught-shut up,
A tough test to pass and sadly there are no make-ups,
In order to truly move these jewels, you shouldn't be scared to see your own blood,

A terrible way to treat gems, but unmoral value systems leads to fewer options,
And when money's your motivation, pearls are the obvious mode of transportation,
Even though the money will just taint you...the erosive effects of degradation,
So if you want to live life on the edge, with snow colored pearls to push your bob-sled,

Know that ~ it ~ in-turn gives you the life of the walking-dead,
No real security when everyone's cross-hairs are aimed for your head,
The life is sweet and sour, good and bad times interchange by the hour,
All for various ounces of, this powerful pearl powder, they store at their pearl-harbor,

I would love to see more buthas get into the real jewelry game,
Clean themselves up and shine like the diamonds in begets setting their chains,
But when you keep seeing the same thangs,
No positive role models make it impossible to leave the game,

So they stick to the pearl-lane, that contains the a.k.a. name, cocaine,
The cop-out frame to put your picture in when on your life is stained or in a strain,
How can you put your life in the hands of something that grows like sugarcane?

Instead of controlling your life-using your brain,
Insanely paranoid, never letting you sleep the same,
Especially knowing another gang's shooters are in range,

It's strange, that someone can place all this stress on themselves,
To chase after riches, not being able to enjoy the paper-trail,
Can't keep saying you didn't know when living life in and out of jail,
At some point there has to be responsibility taken for self,

And the crack game is just the main blue-print out-lined for your life to fail,
It's clearly apparent where the climax is, but the end never wishes you well,
Because when that pearl is the content in the chain that pulls you to pursue,
It ends up controlling like white masters and ultimately hanging you like the noose....

HOMELESS

Where does one dwell,
When the pains of this world swell,
And the fragrance of decrepit, abandonment,
Is the only scent that a nose smells,

Breathing emptiness into an outer shell,
That's been misused and profusely abused,
Causing one to deduce from what they feel,
That "home" is a fictitious word, unreal,

More like a banana peel, causing one to slip,
Into a mist created by their own tears,
Because when ears hear a word like this,
They signal memories someone would resist,

Of something missed in their forsaken life,
So this burn is like a frying bacon slice,
A hidden side that comes with the breakfast served,
So like fast-breaks, one runs out of sight,

To a darkness subconsciously recognized,
As a place that one seemingly knew too well,
The surroundings that tend to spell home,
Now as....H...E...L...L...

Just like an L-Train that's been derailed,
One finds it hard to stay on the right track,
With the feeling of being exiled, as outcasts,
Its hard seeing 1 step, with 2 continually pulling back,

Leading one to never find rest anywhere,
But lay down their head everywhere,
While worrying about each and every care,
Carrying a weight that's too tough to bear,

Though one would love being too tough to scare,
There's still an amount of fear in unsettledness,
A wing and a prayer carrying them along,
As more necessities take the form of a wish,

With this, the only kiss that's received,
Is the cold wind against their cheek,
And being able to eat at all turns into luxury,
Since it may not happen consistently,

All the while one wonder's "are you missing me,
Even though I left with you hitting me,
In an upbeat manner, leaving a beat-up house,
Because I just couldn't endure more of your-beat-downs,"

When one lacks that certain acceptance, of those titled "guardians,"
Teachers that didn't guard against, creating holes instead of a fence,
A formation with a lack of defense, has something eventually taken away,
And often, the most valuable things are the hardest to ever replace,

This house of pain, in the form of a body,
But a connecting heart, mind, and soul, makes it a home,
Thus when one has them as separate entities,
One can never truly know a household,

Or a whole house as a welcoming abode,
Where there once was warm blood, now has turned cold,
So no one will penetrate this remaining ice mold,
Because one froze out the inhabitants, that rent their soul,

Like huge trolls invading these walls, pushing something out,
A childhood, innocence, or the entire good one was about,
Turning all the lights off in a mental museum,
Evicting what was hard to bury, like being deceased in a mausoleum,

So when they kicked out all these memories,
They separated their mind from their heart,
Closing down this battered structure,
Leaving them completely in the dark,

When it was thought that this retraction,
Was the appropriate action, but only in part,
When closing themselves instead of gaining closure,
It internally ripped their build apart…

…Like something cyclonic, which is somewhat ironic,
How an item closed down, implodes from something outside it,
Where heart, mind, and soul had basically collided,
With the fact that they've felt no love that's platonic,

Tough tonic to drink, and a slow pill to swallow,
With unimagined disdain that will also follow,
But the best part of any life submerged in hurt,
Is the prospect that there will eventually come a tomorrow,

With a clean slate, a new state, and laid slab-
Of concrete in your driveway, presenting a new path,
Leading one to eventually find their self,
And turning your house into a home, intact,

While one's mind might have picked up a map,
To choose a spot to run to while the body's attacked,
Don't allow it to wander still helplessly lost,
It always has the urging right to come back,

A soul with no mind, only feels the heart,
Which most times just know to tell the truth,
And since the truth of an aching life is agony,
The body needs the mind to help reduce…

…This misery, to think of hope and see positively,
Only new images one creates, can replace past pictures seen vividly,
If one relives the worst memories of their past,
They'll die never noticing the greener grass,

Even though this outer bodily house,
Can be touched, penetrated, and affected,
Breaking you down into multiple pieces,
Don't let this puzzle remain disconnected,

Being inflected by altering your inner alignment,
Look for a way to stay together, and don't stop till you find it,
If you can't do it alone, find someone to co-sign it,
And if you happen to slip, let this keep you reminded,

That in times with suffering and pain, or joy and happiness,
Whether one dwells with family, friends or alone,
It's irrelevant where you have been placed in this world,
With internal peace as your resident, you're always at home…

Sleep Sight

They say sleep is the cousin of death,
Well dreams are the parents of success,
Your dreams, life's play-written scenes,
The stagehands that construct your set,

This reality-like fantasy-that keeps calling me-
Inspires me-to strive for things that reside in principalities,
Stays in my system like allergies,
But I won't clear up my senses, it's clearer than HD,

Though it drives me crazy,
I'm content with this insanity,
My treasure search to just find a strategy,
To take me to a place I constantly see in my sleep,

This guiding light that stays glowing bright,
Doesn't provide insight, I have to find it on my own,
So I set goals as stepping stones, my own little yellow brick road,
To lead me to this dwelling place that I enjoy so,

And I pursue this mission whole-heartedly,
Since my dream kick-started me-
Imparted on me a view-that's new-
The best uncharted territory,

Not just for the fame and glory,
More for the raw satisfaction of accomplishing something extraordinary,
Because we're much more than a short story,
But more like a biography that's written in series,

A life without dreams is like a past special moment-without memories,
A locked trunk of precious stones, you left alone,
Never looking for the keys,
Because you thought it was impossible for what you've seen to
become a reality,

So your guardians died long ago,
When you found-you'd never be successful,
It's unfortunate that your experiment was never given a trial,
With no imagination you stayed against it like a rival,

When instead your success could have be awaiting your arrival,
Chose to put off your dreams to barely make it through survival,
Because you lack the inspiration-
And negative expectations brought down your elevation,

Seen others dreams deflated, so it's thought their not for you,
Quite the contrary, it's especially for people like you-to improve,
It's easy to be lazy, so simple to lose,
But how much more fulfilling is it to chase-what's seen-when
you snooze,

Not just what's fashionable, or things placed in a muse,
But the things you have passion for-
Embedded deep in you-like burials,
Has the choice to stay dead, or resurrect like those of parables,

To take you to a destination-few work hard enough to reach,
These real-life everyday vacations where your place of work
becomes your beach,
And whatever you see in the mirror you can gladly accept completely,
That's what I imagine is reaching your true destiny,

Not necessarily the screams, flashing & and bright spot-lights,
But the ability to do what you've always shut-eyes visualized,
What you hungered for but never saw on a menu-to do things
never done in a venue,
Something that you naturally just knew, that wasn't outlined with a pencil,

Or copied from using a stencil,
Being the first off the line-creating, being, or doing something new,
So dream on no matter your surroundings,
Don't let that affect your dream's planted groundings,

And though it may be a long road,
Happy is he or she that reaches their goal,
And as you continually go-you happen to experience a
little déjà vu,
Look at it as being a step closer to having all your dreams eventually
come true…

Silent Acts

Violence, the vile pestilence, the element that exist in every facet of life,
So violence is the hood's silence, the unacknowledgement of what isn't right,
Then violence is the suburb's silence, the ignored color-blind hate crimes,
And violence is the militaries silence, when infiltrators cross enemy-lines,

The concept of violent acts being silent is considered pure irony,
But how many mouths have been hushed when lifeless bodies lay quietly,
Violated beloveds now shushed when intruders stole their voice to speak,
Young people seeing things making confused minds, then their teary eyes
are debriefed,

Sheets left with the American colors, of the red, white and blue kind,
Strangled body blue, forced entry red, and erotic stimulant aftermath white,
A terrible sight of a sad reality which leaves us all questioning, why?
If left alive, dumbfounded mothers muffle daughters as their anti-allies,

The frequent occurrence of this practice allows us to keep it on the hush,
Sorry it happened to you sweetheart, but your statistic missed our census,
Persuaded by a mindset lead them to join their generation's caucus,
Two words we think of often, never let up to just ~ shut up ~,

The phrase known well, from street hell, to barred jails,
So this silence helps uplift violence, acting as its handrails,
Leaving these soft dudes on the pavement daily, laying slimy as snails,
And never contemplate the situation, just glad that it wasn't yourself,

For a little money, power, and respect, heataz warm nearby body parts,
Ammunition thrown like darts toward circular targeted boards, which
are hearts,
Silencers from which this poison is tossed, for only pain to impart,
Living lives for the purpose of the next person to possibly out-smart,

A lot of hits-without smoke, a lot of punch lines-missing jokes,
Letting our anger take us much further than anyone should ever travel,
Physical and mental condemnations on the bodies and minds of the fragile,
Then rebellion, revenge, short tempers, and envy cause some to whisper
"die slow,"

On the other side of the globe, using larger weapons, tanks, ships, and aircraft,
Silenced, until the creeping media insects bring terror infested broadcast,
Driven with violent motors, only good news reported if no more bad forecast,
Saving the positive desperately last, no cool fresh breeze of air, just let in a
small draft,

Violence providing the food that audience will constantly feed off,
So silently seeds are spread throughout the world planting mainly this crop,
Few red lights display the sign stop, it's a thought, but without it ratings
would drop,
And this infliction gets sopped up through TV's being used as the mop,

And bought in theater lines, downloaded onto computers through iTunes,
It was said that sex sells, why not add violence to that value,
New kids are looking up to the bad guys silently dropping leaving
empty shoes,
Which they step into quickly, barely hitting puberty, paying street dues,

Trespassed into our schools, as teachers share information building knowledge,
The silent footsteps of violence approaching, to overtake and fundamentally
hold hostage,
Instead destroy the 12 yrs invested, dead-on-arrival cut-short 4 months
before college,
So it's a dream to hit 21, and make it to 18 is becoming a mirage,

Instead of and elemental montage, but violence keeps opening earth's wounds,
Focused on kicking out immigrants, since violence wont leave, scoot
over-make room,
Silence so loud-blocks positivity like clouds-
But green comes from this bile, thrown in our salads like mushrooms,
All the while knowing this quiet instrument decomposes life's beautiful tune,

No noise heard from the abused, locked up, and departed cadavers
And rarely do we address the problem that causes this terrible matter,
Chit-chatter, that's rarely productive, makes our society move slowly down
the ladder,
Stillness inside, still thrives, thinking it will naturally leave like waste out
of bladders,

Until it's identified as a blaring sound, roaring from the underground's jagged
crust,
Ignoring simply because, it hasn't had a chance to directly affect us,
But this silence arises steadily in faces like a new day's dose of fresh dust,
And will continue, until the word before ***up*** is replaced with ***step*** and not ***shut***...

The Essentials

I need you like the soil, sun, and water that nurtures a seed,
To instill values, brighten my day, and quench my thirst for life refreshingly,
Keeping me deeply rooted, so that I'll stay continually grounded,
And the negative surroundings won't affect me because this shield won't let me be around it…

Always remembering from which I was founded,
How I was shaped and-formed-and obstacles I bounded,
Just because you were in the corner of my square, in the radius of my inner circle,
And the hidden weapon in my lair,

So my need for you is essential as air,
Like the kid reaching for cookies,
You'd be my chair,
But I'd never hold back, always willing to share,

Because I need you like a pen needs paper,
To let me vent, record my thoughts, and believe my stories,
And though I may never be a famous writer,
hearing you say "its ok" does everything for me,

Never judging what I speak,
being the paper towel that cleaned up my leak,
Keeping it contained so what's said,
won't spread, like the water of a broken sink,

When troubled waters I crossed, you were the boat that kept me afloat,
Keeping me in check like the square on the ballot to vote,
The heimlich that never let me choke,
And kept the focus at the clearest setting on my scope,

Building me up, strengthening me,
Encouraging and giving me wisdom,
Being the one to uplift me, even if it takes criticism,
But it's always given constructively, without the added cynicism,

You're the bail and I'm the innocent man in prison,
There when I need you most,
And won't brag, boast, or throw in my face,
All the times you've brought me out the heat, like toast,

Even when my life was up and down like rollers that coast,
The prescription you gave was the accurate dose,
Because you had my back, wasn't on it, like a book-bag,

Any weight overloaded, you helped toss out like dirty rags,
And once let go you were never the bum that dug in the trash,
You said to keep looking forward,
Can't stay on path continually looking back,

The revelations you passed have turned the light on in dark rooms,
So in my town with few street lights, you'd be my full moon,
Can barely remember your nuisance in my lawn like mushrooms,
You were the fresh water stream, and not that salty lagoon,

You constantly add to my being, making me a better person,
Though beatings come in life,
You smooth it over, never worsened,
The stress reliever when I'm burdened,

Being my co-pilot to help me steer
When you feel my life is turning,
My hunger that keeps on yearning, not to settle for less,
The maid that provided aid, to clean up my dirty mess,

Then keeping me on key,
By serving as the markings on the lines next to the treble clef,
Finding in my life's masterpiece,
My director only accepts excellence,

Because I've learned from experience, that I can't make it by myself,
And I don't want to be the toy, alone, collecting dust on the shelf,
The added companionships and relationships...
Serve as a needed ingredient to the fruits of labor I dish,

So looking back on my life, my reality is...I need you...

Father, mother, sister, brother,
Teacher, preacher, and the congregational leaders,
My friends, my family, my girl, wife-or to be,
My co-workers, my associates, and my boss working with me,
My fellas that make it rain, my girls that bring out the umbrellas,
My elders, and even my hater's, always ready to point out my failures,

Because life alone, is like the astronaut on the moon,
Without the added comfort of having a spaceship to fly home,
And the harmony from a group is impossible to make on your own,

With the phone-line disconnected, you only get a dial-tone,
Because the essentials are that everyone needs someone,
With-out the added insight, you'll never be what you could become....

THE FAM

A relationship that will forever surpass,
All acquaintances, contacts, and associations,
These persons have high regard, upper class,
Even when not labeled in society, that's our consideration,

Our connection stays irrevocable,
A binding contract, signed timeless, by both parties,
So even in times when we become unsociable,
They still hold me down completely, never half-heartedly,

A large part of me, finds commonality,
"Like the birds of a feather"…or "when in Rome"…
Home is where the heart is, a known generality,
So wherever we sit, we're still on our thrones,

In a kingdom surrounding our round table,
So these pawns won't infiltrate our inner circle,
The entrance to that door is, for most, unattainable,
And we won't advertise it like its commercial,

Like the chains of inmates stuck on death row,
We're pretty much in this thing for life,
But these chains are heart strings, from where the blood flows,
Which is impossible to cut, no matter the knife,

Even in drama episodes, they're like the cast and crew,
There to back me up, and keep my character tight,
Although, we rarely act…well wait, we sometimes fool,
After that we pull it together, cuz, we know how to get right…

With each other, or another, whenever someone flips the script,
Telling the truth, whether or not that's something you want to hear,
Bringing you back to reality, and off that high horse quick,
If you get caught up with your boo, looks, money, or career,

But after the moods, tears, fights and heated arguments,
You still have love for your folk, A.K.A…your people,
They're the ones on your side, of the transparent limo tints,
Because behind closed doors, no one will see you as they do,

So we call them "The Fam," related in blood or spirit,
A support group never too far to answer any beck and call,
And anyone who disrespected will come to fear it,
If you didn't know, when you get one, trust, you got us all,

That's as it should be, confident that they will always be there,
But there's also too many examples of loved ones, found slippin',
Fathers gone missin', abusive relationships, and few that care,
The type of pain that is healed without any prescription,

Because a cut from an alleged family member,
Makes you view them more as a guest, uncommitted,
Making your feelings change toward them, like seasons in September,
A genetic structure doesn't always keep individuals closely knitted,

Even though, an ancestry bloodline suggest we relate,
It, by no means, automatically places you in "The Fam,"
If you don't come real, represent, or your loyalty is up for debate,
You're just not in correlation with who I am,

How many adoption agencies, now fill spots on family trees,
Or day cares witnessing moment's intermediate families should share,
A teacher who gave the most support when guardians didn't believe,
Or friends that helped defend when no siblings were there,

No piece of paper proves to a person, who they relate to,
Many have that confused; your significance must run deeper,
It's really about what I see…and more so, what you do,
Inclining me to stay up with you, or on your title, become a sleeper,

Though the choice is uncontrolled of your inherited bloodline,
Who stays in your presence, is always something you choose,
The question of will we stay tight, or in time, unwind,
Depends on how high family sits on your list of values,

Thankfully I cherish the ones I've been given,
For never dropping the landing gear of my elevated expectations,
Even in the times when, up the wall, I've been driven,
I wouldn't have anyone else ride as I reach my destination,

I can say I know what true family is, and should be,
A blessing, the total opposite of anything resembling strife,
So to my people, my friends, my loved ones, "THE FAM,"
I say with all sincerity much love and respect, for life…

Street College

It's interesting how I dropped out of high school,
Only to still make it into college;
That street college-where learning is crucial-
And acceptance letters are received unpolished,
The recruiters were smooth, providing prime examples,
Of the ending result when closely following the manual,
The manual; though there's many-
To become playa's, pimps, gangsta's, and hustla's,
There's a code between all,
Valued higher than all the others,
That's the curriculum we're taught to live-by,
And die-for if need-be,
Graphs are only drawn 3D,
Samples of cats X'd out, asking Y, catching Z's,
The realistic examples prepare us students quickly,

So we can walk the hallways with poise,
Instead of ending up ajar,
And fear is an odor that's smelled from afar,
Which we're taught to not show from the start,
You find classmates to group with eventually,
Finding it's smart to roll with a crew,
A couple with the same mentality,
And a couple to use as your goons,
Handed a utensil filled with lead,
Though it was not a #2,
More like a 9, 22, 44, or 45 caliber,
And we upgrade the more we get comfortable,

Our paper sits outside of binders and folders,
In large amounts-its n duffle bags,
In short stacks-we fold it over,
Learn to count money on your own,
Motivation for that comes easily,
The difference is weighing and cutting products up right,
Then breaking them down evenly,
Don't act on nothing greedily,
That's a sure way to eventually fail,
Slow motion, like boat sails,
Often propels you best to get wealth,

And mail street credit to our registrar,
To keep us in these classes,
So return on all loans well approved,
Or your new dorm is filled with ashes,
Report cards either inspire tattoos,
Or are attached with particle lodges and scars,
If you get frustrated by your reviews,
Placed those diffused feelings in a jar,
Learn to store your bruised egos,
Then make your victims feel your pain,
Cuz if you drop out of this game,
Liquor hits the pavement while saying your name,

And neva-eva-eva tell,
Neva-eva let secrets go,
If you get caught on the hook,
Be the fish with its mouth closed,
Because in too many experiments-
We've seen all types of rodents dissected,
"Rats" are the most popular subject,
They squeal no matter how their directed,
We learn to lie with straight faces,
The truth isn't only what'll hurt you,
Our teacher's may be knowledge spitta's,
But they know how to do dirt too,

It's kill or be killed, eat or be eaten,
And stay with the heat in spite of the season,
If people wonder why we're made hard,
That's mainly the reason,
Doggy-dog world we live in,
With junkyard-like surroundings,
So if it wasn't for our mentoring life-guards,
We'd be in the sea-of-life drowning,
Cuz I searched through the catalog,
And not once did I see daddy classes,
Since most enter this way,
The masses are correct when they call us bastards,

That's why we rarely can respect women,
No love for ourselves, just love the wealth,
And unless you talking money,
My ears can't seem to pick-up nothing else,
So green is our favorite color,
Like we stepped out of Ireland,
Irish dreams of gaining those means,
To stay fly like peter pan,
So our school for lost boys,
Keep us with tools-grown man toys,
Use them to drill-like in woodshop class,
Though it delivers a snare-drum noise,

Leaving our enemies burning-like mouths with altoids,
And watch with no remorse,
Because overall we're taught to use brute force,
Just down the wrong course,
You see-we learn what's placed in front of us,
Like pigs learn to eat what's placed in their pail,
But sadly the thought-process we're shown,
Just teaches us in the end to fail,

We can evaluate colors like an artist,
And cook "it" up like the best culinary chefs,
Keep a close eye on the money like accountants,
And hand out whoopins like those with black belts,
We can motivate each other easily,
Like any of the famous oratorical speakers,
And know the animal kingdom of the ghetto,
Like zoologist we study hood creatures,
And those that carry themselves with more class,
We analyze like we in anthropology,
Scanning your thoughts like psychology,
And cracking ya'll lil codes like cryptology,
With ya'll lil stereotypical ideology,
Thinking ya'll rule over us like aristocracy,
But in the end we tryna be hood stars,
So we all into astronomy,

We got some religion-we oppose hospitals like the scientologist,
So we map out our surroundings like cartologist,
Research your historic where-abouts like paleontologist,
And let our street sweepers dust you off like archaeologist,
Stretching out infiltrators like physical therapist,
Then telling the story like a journalist,
Keep taking names out the game,
And placing them on mortician's list,
We learn the ins and outs of the hood,
Like we're trained auto mechanics,
Get fluent in a couple languages,
Using linguistics to transmit,
When in transit-we move like postal and parcel workers,
Don't send postal cards,
But get the big picture like we dark-room photographers,
Start our own operations,
Built from the ground-up like an entrepreneur,
And learn to critic like we're the best-
Of any type of connoisseur,

So calling us dumb is far-from-
The education that comes in our eyes and ear-drums,
Instead of ya'll nice lil college towns,
We're set to learn in the slums,
While ya'll walk the stage to receive degrees,
We get ours if we can still breathe,
We learn well, we're no different,
Just got negative teachers to lead,
Taking out the time to invest in me,
Since public systems are quick to leave,
So the only success we've seen,
Are those with pockets full of cheese,

Our brains as powerful as-
The Washington-Carvers and Martin-Luther's
But our environment lacks the positive types of tutors,
Ignorance; not stupidity,
Not forced to focused; which they call ADD,
When I happen to not learn as fast,
They pass judgment on me,
All types of books to read, -ologist to be,
And information we could study
But when it comes to lower class living,
Educators can't seem to prepare me properly,
Like all of a sudden they've forgot how to teach,

Are they scared of what I'll be?
That I'll make a bigger mark in history?
That if I'm lead to the water,
It creates less room for them to drink?
So I'm fed tap water out the sink,
Instead of fresh water out wells and streams,
And instead of inspecting,
I'm left the target of most crime scenes,

If I don't learn what you know,
How can I be better than you?
So they keep a lil bread circulating,
Quietly funding our street school,
Because they know our potential,
The ability to go above and beyond,
But we still working ghetto plantations,
The block as our new farm,
When knowledge is power,
A communication that always transcends,
Without it we're ending our means,
Instead of having a means to an end….

The Cropped Image

There are ones found in water,
Opposite that of Lake Superior,
They are seen instead drowning,
In the seas labeled "Inferior"

Consistently changing things on the exterior,
While their interior truly needs decoration,
Quiet as kept, they want to be him, her, or them,
Thinking of themselves as a lower form of creation,

Lacking the affirmations that are essential,
That would bring success into their lives,
Because they've too been given the exact same things,
As the persons they dream of and idolize,

So rather than rise, they sink in backgrounds,
And just watch, as opposed to taking action,
Because this looks too hard, and that rubs the wrong way,
But without any friction, nothing would ever gain traction

Sadly, not using a fraction of the talent bestowed,
They'll use or be used, demoralize themselves, or won't attempt-
Anything at all that would be worthwhile,
Since their mental judge keeps them in their own contempt,

They seem to just rent the frame they embody,
Not fully taking ownership of the things they're given,
These amazing skills and qualities wanting to be tapped,
But stay undiscovered like unknown stars in a solar system,

Not trying to show symptoms, some fake it-to make it,
Overcompensating this lack of self worth that's felt,
Saying all these outrageous things that they probably could do,
But whenever it's crunch time, that front just always seems to melt,

In that sweltering heat that comes from pressure,
Or the spotlights being aimed at a stage,
Even the little things daily that make them choose to settle,
This feeling of incompetence, just keeps them afraid,

Like a young man's rage, feeling there's something to prove,
Based off someone that abused, hurt, or belittled him in the past,
Now mad at the innocent world, with uncontrollable pain,
Walking around with an intimidation factor as a mask,

Waking each new morning asking yet again,
In the end, was that person's implication actually right?
But if he truly knew himself, he'd live without doubt,
With no need for confirmations in these numerous fights,

With insight he would conquer himself, through an internal war,
Knowing words can hurt, but more-so, the one's we speak over ourselves,
Actions leave scars, however significant, we also leave our own wounds,
This pent up anger, never prevails, just builds impetuous carousels,

Whereas a frail young lady worries late through night,
Silently trying to convince herself she's not stupid,
Instead just helpless in, what she wants to call love,
With a man acting as if his middle name was cupid,

So rather than lose it, she'll comply with sharing,
Since her rational says, "Men all cheat anyway,"
But possibly its penetration cuts much deeper,
Thinking she might be inadequate to cause him to stay,

She'll act OK with half of something, instead of all of nothing,
His words make her feel like the leading actress in a play,
The same type of things she could easily tell herself,
But doesn't know how or won't, keeping him around anyway,

Using what's between her legs, rather than that between her ears,
Under the impression that having his baby, will cause him to stick,
This eternal attachment-not as strong as a person loving the true you,
If she had relied on her strengths, he may have chosen to commit,

If not him, then someone equipped to better handle her,
She being sure of herself will keep her focus completely straight,
Knowing that she deserves the best treatment, with the highest respect,
Though physically she's alone, the right mate is worth the wait,

Additionally, these haters who try and negate, all positive success,
On-lookers, always waiting for a shooting star to fall short,
Wanting to feel better about themselves, they hope to see others fail,
But will always be disgusted, when to those low standards, we won't resort,

They observe and report, on everything someone else is doing,
In the shadow of their spotlight, consistently criticizing,
Comfortable in the audience, where risk is non-existent,
What these stars do every day, they can only do when fantasizing,

Not realizing, these gifts aren't just handed, but relentlessly worked for,
The long hours, tedious practice, the behind closed door commotion,
This unseen transformation results an internal rejuvenation,
So it never really affects us, them taking shots at our old emotions,

When the door opens, these haters see an equivalent image,
But the cover of the book never reveals the inner magnitude,
The esteem that never lifted them to a higher stage in life,
Causes them to invite us to visit a lower altitude,

But those who refuse, know that attitude is everything,
Wearing it daily like a wedding ring, to show their fidelity,
With confidence in their gifts, still willing to step out with courage,
Not letting failure immobilize them from moving ahead readily,

Still pedaling through this world that's always turning,
Whether a pair of feet are moving or not,
So is there steam churning the desires inside you?
Or has it left you no fuel, paralyzing you, stopped?

Have you cropped the image of yourself, with no software?
Lacking self-belief, with unrevealed talents,
Not valuing the life that's been given every new day,
Without aiming toward your potential, your life just hangs in the balance,

Not being able to sit in palace surroundings,
For we all were truly born as kings and queens,
Be confident in your identity, never wandering fully substandard-
Serving as a peasant in the desolate land of Low Self-Esteem..

THE LANGUAGE OF WORDS UNSAID

There is a language of words unsaid,
Traveling to my head from the heart,
Though seemingly silent, they swim in my blood,
To touch each one of my body parts,

From the depths of my very soul,
Through my nerves, valves, canals, and veins,
To my feet and hands, but resting in my head,
Then out the mouth if released from my brain,

But when I actually speak it is unheard,
Instead it's made visual for you to see,
Because when I choose to unleash these words,
They paint the picture of the real me,

With colors of my memory, the present, and my future,
Since my past influenced where I am presently,
This present, not always handed out nicely wrapped,
But how it's opened-effects my future significantly,

Not equivocally but more specifically,
Do these words outline the contours of my frame,
Like painters sketching live nude models,
Being completed with my artistically signed name,

But this is only when this literature is released,
Like best selling novels off my internal shelves,
If not, it continually swells, spreading throughout,
It seeps through all organs, penetrating all cells,

So all I smell is incensed with good "sense,"
Making everything I touch eventually prevail,
Causing everything I see to be viewed positively,
And what I hear is scanned more thorough than inmate's mail,

All because the things that I say aloud,
Align with my body before their released from my lips,
So even when you receive signals silently,
It's still all honesty that you get,

Not letting me switch in split seconds,
Because my mentalities are highly solidified,
Directing the way that this substance flows,
So my mind is the moon controlling this tide,

A pull acting gravitational, but more inspirational,
Handing you sensational effects in whatever I do…
And sometimes say, as my balance is revealed between the 2,
So my stance on different things never has you confused,

As these 3 words extend to all my limbs,
And continuously play my organs in the right key,
My hands and feet work properly, and then unify,
So when I utter "I Love You" my actions agree,

Which doesn't allow me to show you anything opposite,
My hands won't ball up in fist, tightened only to hit,
My legs won't bend to my knees, placing me always out on the creep,
Nor my feet sliding on ice, skating around you all slick,

It would instead make me the nest that safely holds my chick,
A silence that connects us like stapled documents,
Then even when my anger turns me off, like unignited starters,
Correlating actions back my past words, like the 6th man on the bench,

Not on the fence when anyone mentions the term respect,
Because it's all about what you inject and not what you interject,
It's seeing, feeling, smelling, and tasting…that, which I gave you,
So upon hearing me say "I Respect You" you're unable to object,

Since it just makes that much sense…
I wouldn't be able to convince anyone with just my voice,
I actually have that type of poise that stays attached,
Therefore it's not falsely represented, displayed like decoys,

I can't kill that noise, when we're referencing loyalty,
As long as I'm the one you still see standing when the smoke clears,
Always there right beside you, when your fears thought you were abandoned,
So when I announce "I'll Always Be Loyal" your heart knew before your ears,

Clearly making me trustworthy to rely on,
When trust might have been the hardest thing someone could do,
I remained hard too, like an anchor holding you down,
Hence your memory's vivid imagery as evident proof,

It's uncouth to say courage does not reside inside of me,
If strength leaks through my aura, and defeat I won't accept,
With each step I take, that's forward, in the valley of the shadow of death,
Makes the statement "I'm Courageous,"
a vocal acknowledgement you won't reject,

Placing me constantly in a leadership position,
With this passion, relentless nature, and my tenacity,
Because I stepped up to the plate, when everyone seemed against me,
Which isn't recognized by just titles, but what's seen in my qualities,

And if I happen to cough and sneeze, my body's removing impurities,
So that I only have internal strings keeping me genuinely sincere,
Thus what you see-is what you get, I won't split from my identity,
Consequently when it's vocalized "I'm Real,"
I'm no farmer giving you manure from a bull's rear…

Meaning I did not choose the career as a fictitious novel writer,
What the mirror shows me, is the exact reflection that these words created,
Making all my stories true, or based in some way off fact,
So that my image lives in your mind, and doesn't lie there cremated,

Decoding my image into 1,000 words that you'll still hear,
In view of a picture being at least that much,
Each stroke from this paint brush is drawn correct,
Making this authenticity never able to fade, so I can never lose touch,

Making me more than just clutch, in any game situation,
Because my consistency convinced you to be a believer,
No matter how the circumstances and variables were ever mixed up,
The result of the experiment is always the same in this beaker,

This then makes me meeker, watching the things that I choose to say,
Knowing that these words not only be heard but pictured in equaled amounts,
So if I speak less to foolish people on subjects not made to edify,
It's just that I consider myself bound to the things I pronounce,

With an ounce of inconsistency, the masses then begin to doubt,
Like stains, it's hard to clear your name, saying things you don't fulfill,
I instead hand you a stethoscope to listen to my heart through auscultation,
Keeping my status at the same amount of that Benjamin Franklin dollar bill,

Yet still…many of you may wonder "what is language of unsaid words,"
They are words of life that literally take up structure and then walk,
They speak to all sizes, ages, genders in addition to colors alike,
It is in every way, shape, and form what most of us call "Real Talk…"

The Real Evolution...

For those of you who've never heard it,
We know the real Evolution,
It all started with God,
Despite what's taught in these institutions,

HE created the heavens, the earth,
The stars and everything in between,
Then came the elements of life...
The plants, creatures, Adam and his queen,

Adam's job was received,
At the very beginning of his story...
To name the animals, side-note; for scientist,
I'm sure apes were in his inventory,

Eve was also given a purpose,
As the compelling companion to man,
The one to assist at his side,
As they fulfilled god's plan,

From these two came many generations,
Some names you may know well,
Like Joseph, one of the best worker's ever-
Purchased on sale,

His purpose was to translate dreams,
And sustain his land and legacy,
Even though jail was a place he'd see-
Before He could reach his destiny,

This opened a door into the Canaan Land
Where Joshua led the children of Israel,
But before the promise was fulfilled,
They had to conquer a task seeming abysmal,

This soon brought a man-after god's own heart,
Who defeated Goliath with a stone,
As a mighty man of valor,
Though David too-had to repent for all his wrongs,

Eventually there came Ester the queen-
Unable to reveal her true kindred,
But had she not appealed to the king,
They would've erased her entire lineage,

All serving as major steps-
In the heritage of how we're saved,
Because they all led to Jesus' death,
Making the church what it is today,

Though there were many along the way,
All these stories were chosen for a reason,
Because at an early age,
The lord was molding each of them for their own season,

Joseph was a teenager when he was sold to slavery,
But that's what positioned him to be blessed,
Though Joshua wasn't young when he saw Canaan,
He led a movement aging 20 and less,

David was too a young man
When he visualized that Giant defeated,
And Ester was a young lady becoming queen,
Before she even knew how much she would be needed,

Then came along a man named Jesus,
Who's youth was an important part of his fate,
His death was undoubtedly indispensable,
But his father's business started at an early age,

With these stories, combined and streamlined,
We are able to jump to the present,
Where God is still wrapping our youth up with gifts,
Like we're all our parents' presents,

Though if you've ever seen a gift unwrapped,
The transition is not always neat,
But like carnivores scrape past the fur of their prey,
The good stuff is much further than skin-deep,

What I'm saying is we're not all perfect,
And oftentimes our path is hard to grasp,
But like god never left his children in the wilderness,
We need your support until we reach greener grass,

So I repeat, we know the real evolution-
Because we too must evolve,
From the days we were a sinner…
To the days we're no longer involved,

So I welcome you to the church of transformers,
Because God's not done with us yet...
We're still running this race to win,
Even if not prepared, at the "ready, set..."

For those who don't like it,
Hate all you want-but you'll never stop me,
And you can doubt me if u feel led to,
But trust me, I'm no copy,

My story is too original,
To be compared to those I resemble,
If you thought you'd predict my end-by how I started,
I'm sorry it's not that simple,

So again I say-welcome, but this time,
It's to the future,
For in this church sits perspective doctors,
Lawyers, teachers, and tutors...

Preachers, accountants, engineers, presidents,
And meteorologist for the weather,
And if we fall short of your standards,
Maybe you used the wrong ruler to measure,

Because we're young, enthusiastic, and boisterous,
And we'll reach our purpose one day,
In the meantime if we have a little fun,
Don't take life so serious; none make it out alive anyway....

But pray...that we'll grow,
Into the men and women we're meant to be,
As soldiers following the true commander,
Not a fan watching from a court-side seat...

The President

There is one patriot, who's chosen to lead
A country; home to the brave and land of the free
Using passion, relentless efforts, and strong determination
As fuel, burning the desire to watch his homeland succeed.

A flame symbolized in a torch shining so bright
That liberty and justice for all remains at his foresight
Through long days, and dark nights, his 20/20 remains futuristic
Unlike televisions, showing a 20/20 that enlarges our plight.

He wavers not in the eyes of the press, nor in the face of terror
Whether he encounter one or both amidst any decision or endeavor
And if the dark clouds of failure loom, he warrants us to ascend
Hoping his people never cease viewing with indulgence, his errors.

For honesty is the best policy not a deceptive manipulation
Public faith in the integrity of his office, takes priority over all his consideration
An integrity that must be real, since "the people" deserve truthfulness
Bearing this responsibility, he gains trust, as the head of any organization.

A trust not only in him, but in an ideal that's much greater,
That an infinite power which rules the universe, leads his council with favor,
Acknowledging and adorning an overruling providence, and all its delights,
In the happiness of men-women-boys-and-girls alike, whether now or later.

Stemming from the root of freedom, which grants the ability to choose,
And with such freedom, comes also those few, who would negatively abuse-
Those privileges, rights, laws, and rules, in a way that's meant to undermine
But just like an underline, he upholds the words he swore never to misuse.

Believing freedom and security go together,
to strengthen Liberty and World Peace,
So even on the front lines, he stands confident-ready to fight for its upkeep
Proud of a nation privileged to spend blood
and might for principles that gave her birth,
Making him unable to weep long for soldiers who carnally pass-on deceased.

For their memory will never die; he ensures that it suffers no corrosion
With increased dedication to that cause for which
they gave the last full measure of devotion
So the dead-die not in vain, rather their bloodshed runs in a nation's veins
With a leader able to transfuse their loss with uplifting emotion.

Through an unmistakable sound, ringing out like bells from a steeple
His voice, because the connection with each of his countrymen is equal
And we cannot be separated in interest nor ever divided by purpose
When titles differentiate us, his example is the glue uniting his people.

As a teacher, daily spreading knowledge to those who are willing to listen
The chef, working with multicolor ingredients in a melting pot kitchen
A musician, knowing nothing's better than life played out in harmony
The salesman, working to gain participation, through his earnest commission.

As a student continually learning, since knowledge
only expands your perception
The judge, making decisions that affect us for life,
that often facilitate correction
An architect, maintaining a structure that is renovated by the times
The soldier, willing to die for our beliefs, fight for our rights,
and kill for our protection.

As an engineer, staying abreast of the
many technological advancements
The philanthropist, giving to others following the golden rule commandment
A teller bringing change to appease the elders,
and support the newer generation
And the artist seeing us as works of art, filling this world with enchantment.

For when we ask not what this country can do for us,
but what we can do for this country
And focus not on making a leader fall, like he was
nicknamed Humpty Dumpty
We stand together as the brightest beacon for freedom
and opportunity in the world
Even if the historic road paved behind us may have been laid a little bumpy.

We should look forward to what we've been given,
and not focus on what we lack
Build up the inhabitants in our own habitats, without the ill-will to ransack
Unleashing the greatness that lies within,
despite all opposition trying to deter
Success is not the measure of a man but a triumph
over those who choose to hold him back.

We must not only seek for change, but that we must also create
And yet again the torch changes hands for a new generation
to lead in a way that's great
But only one steps out as Head of State, Commander and Chief,
the national CEO
It is, has been, and always will be, ***The President of the United States.***

My Prayer

Lord,
Keep my over-rationalization,
From blocking your deep revelation.
Keep my need for only the explicable,
From blocking the sight of your marvelous miracles.
Keep my lust of temporary pleasures,
From blocking the values of heavenly treasures.
And Keep my lingering double-minded thoughts,
From blocking my ascent to these mountaintops.

Lord,
Keep the fear of sanctification,
From blocking the light of my illumination.
Keep the pressure of my closest peers,
From blocking the morals that I hold dear.
Keep all these sins and negative habits,
From blocking your teachings; that's paradigmatic.
And Keep the following of news and gossip,
From blocking your footsteps for me to be apostolic.

Lord,
Keep the words that slip out in profane ways,
From blocking blessings-so curses don't ricochet.
Keep ***the*** internal reluctance ***I have*** to forgive,
From blocking your grace when I don't rightly live.
Keep the fragments of my broken heart,
From blocking the line you've drawn, saying "restart."
And Keep the feelings of this empty soul,
From blocking your will for me to be whole.

For without the help of an almighty Lord,
I am just a man in discord.
Not fervently searching for life with harmony,
Unaware of this-cord-I live carnally.
Driven by my impulse or fleshly feeling,
And not how my true spirit is willing;
As sheep wandering beyond the Shepherds reach,
Unprotected from a Devil, who waits to breech-

Any area that I convey the sign weak,
To destroy me in a way that's not at all discrete.
See, he'd too love to use me as an example,
Another one of God's chosen-he easily trampled.
But I was made to be a trampoline for Christ,
Causing those to leap in faith, elevate, and take flight.
So Father, my prayer asks-that you remain my Savior,
To strengthen me daily, if ever I waver…

Lord,
So the faith which shields me as I embark,
Keeps blocking the attacks of fiery darts.
So the salvation that's placed on my head,
Keeps blocking spiritual traps the wicked spread.
So the whole armor you supplied,
Keeps blocking the evil wiles the Devil tried.
So the countless Angels providing provision,
Keep blocking the demons who cause division.

Lord,
So the doors you've closed in my life,
Keep blocking all paths except the way that's right.
So the hills, where I set my eyes,
Keep blocking the valley where rivers of tears lie.
So the strength given to do all things,
Keeps blocking the limits previously seen.
So the renewed mind I transformed,
Keeps blocking the influence to conform.

Lord,
So the trust I have in your presence,
Keeps blocking the things that are irreverent.
So the word hidden within my heart,
Keeps blocking immoral things the world would impart.
So the peace passing all understanding,
Keeps blocking the symptoms-stress is demanding.
Ultimately, so my intense love for you,
Keeps blocking the ability to be swayed by how others do.

So that I might be seen as your child,
Whether standing in or out the crowd.
Whether under bright or stormy skies,
Whether life or death, sink or rise.
Whether elements are in or out of my control,
Whether those I called friends come or go.
My steadfast hope lies in you alone,
For there's none other, and no one can clone...

The true and living God, the one I love,
Who the moon, sun, and stars-sits above
Watching my every move with precision,
And has an open ear always to listen,
That any prayer might be heard,
If I just open my heart and speak the word.
So to the master holding my life, ever-so
delicately in his hand,
This will forever be my prayer...in Jesus Name, Amen...

FOR MY LADY

I wonder can you handle it
Or are you good enough to dismantle it.
Are you hotter than fireplace mantles get
Or that much colder than icebergs sit?
Either way, you probably could get you a piece-
Only if you hate drama and love the peace.
If my Love's what you hunger-gone and eat,
Fulfil your appetite with a course of me.

Let things proceed, taking its course
Extend me your time with no remorse,
Can you feel my words smoothly enter your pores
Kind-of refreshing...you like how it pours?
Well, I'm told, that I contain a craft
That easily compliments your smile and laugh.
Compliments to the creator-for you-I'll add...
and I gotta say, I'm loving that math…

...Not equations subtracting your underwear
-Though still deep penetration getting under...where...
Fragile places are shown with no despair
Since I handle with care, like no parcel service compares
And serve-is something I do for my lady
You'll want for nothing, well... double portions, maybe
Others want to rock that boat, sign you up for the Navy
I'd rock your world as you dream, cradling my baby

If you ask what I see with you
…Well...Mainly the future, like horoscopes do,
No whore-I-scope when focusing you in my view
Just hope that image stays still, motion pictures ensue...
There's an actress in my presence, but an actor's not me
Too many people already act-or front like reality TV
I'll only picture you in the real world, like the paparazzi
So if you like this ideal, we'll kick it like karate...

Primarily...I-deal with the best
Like a new deck of cards to gambling guest
I relate to a Casino-but don't be distressed
Be-cause-see-no brotha has you this impressed

Plus there's a gamble trying someone new,
Separating the real from those just trying to woo
But by the time I'm done I want you thinking "woooo!"
From how my class-like transparency revealed to you...

That there's still a few guys-seeing women as prize...
And in this day and time, that's seen as a surprise
But you'll find I'm too original-to wear a disguise,
A stand up dude among many, choosing a position that lies
But in here still lies...my question,
can you handle this perception?
...Or can you dismantle-causing inception,
placing your dream within mine-without interception?

Seeing that, we all basically chase the same thing...
a good catch, but...without intersecting
Our happiness; that's the catch-keeping our grass always green,
so on no other side will we be found visiting
See...most visualize greener grass from the outside looking in,
using their visual-eyes to compare their current condi-tion
But from the ground-up-inside out, is how love should begin,
where windows of the soul just see the greener grass we tend

Making our outlook tend-to-see brighter,
not left in the dark-no all nighter-
Call me Old Faithful, like that geyser,
because I commit when most of these guys-are...
...Not...
But that's the least I can do for my lady,
even when it gets hard-in Thunder like OKC-
She'll understand when I smile and say "every-thing's OK...See?"
Because through whateva we'll stick together like the insides of pastry

Prepared to see that ribbon in the sky-as our rainbow
And no, won't join that coalition to help her see that rainbow
There'll be no worries about my standards
          lowering to a level "downlow..."
Even if "sex" goes unmentioned we'll
          still see good things develop slow...
Yea, I know-dudes might call me slow, for not always tryna hit
And chicks might be in ya ear about how biological clocks tick
But they don't get..how..life becomes a constant climax,
          when you live this eclec-tic
Well, reaching the climax is better than telling so
          - we'll leave them all as scep-tics

Until then…let's give them something to
talk about like Bonnie Raitt...
And if ever second rate dudes advance,
you'd easily say "I'm straight"
Since you allowed me to advance when you saw I
held substantial weight
And even if that's not today, it's coo, for my lady is worth the wait...

J U S T D O I T

I used to run from the hurt,
Until my gain outweighed the pain.
Used to hate the demands of practice,
Until it paid off in the game

I used to fear my competition,
Until I noticed fear in their eyes.
Used to shy away from a challenge,
Until my talent gave me pride.

I used to think failure could stop me,
Until those hard times paved my way.
Used to reside in the shadows,
Until spotlights placed me on display.

I used to listen to all my critics,
Until they were drowned out by my heart.
Used to harshly judge humble beginnings,
But my end won't resemble the start…

…Really…

I USED to JUST dream,
Until my dreams started coming true.
So I no longer JUST wish…
Now…I JUST DO…

Appendix i

References:

For the poem entitled "The President." (In order of use)

Line 12 – President George Washington
Line 14 – President Richard Nixon
Line 18/19 – President Thomas Jefferson
Line 25 – President Ronald Reagan
Line 27 – President Woodrow Wilson
Line 30 – President Abraham Lincoln
Line 35 – President Woodrow Wilson
Line 49 – President John F. Kennedy
Line 51 – President George W. Bush
Line 56 – President Bill Clinton
Line 57 – President Barack Obama

Montefiore, S. S. (2005). Speeches that changed the world.
London: Quercus Publishing Plc.

Washington, G. (Sept. 17, 1796). 'A passionate attachment of one nation for another produces a variety of evils.' Farewell Address.

Nixon, R. M. (April 30, 1973). 'There can be no whitewash at the White House.' Address to the Nation.

Jefferson, T. (March 4, 1801). 'We are all Republicans, we are all Federalist.' Inaugural Address

Reagan, R. (June 12, 1987). 'Mr Grobachev, tear down this wall. ' Speech at the Brandenburg Gate: Berlin.

Wilson, W. (April 2, 1917). 'The world must be made safe for democracy. 'Speech to Congress

Lincoln, A. (Nov. 19, 1863). 'Four score and seven years ago our fathers brought forth on this continent a new nation…' The Gettysburg Address

Kennedy, J. F. (Jan. 20, 1961) 'Ask not what your country can do for you; ask what you can do for your country.' Inaugural Address

Bush, G. W. (Sept. 11, 2001). 'A great people has been moved to defend a great nation.' Address to the nation.

- Clinton, W. J. (Motivational Quote - Date N/A). "Success is not the measure of a man, but a triumph over those who choose to hold him back." http://thinkexist.com/quotation/success_is_not_the_measure_of_a_man_but_a_triumph/151094.html
- Thum, M. (2008, para. 12 {#2. Change}). 'Top 10 of Barack Obama Quotes of Change.' http://www.myrkothum.com/top-10-of-barack-obama-quotes-of-change/

www.ingramcontent.com/pod-product-compliance
Lightning Source LLC
LaVergne TN
LVHW051608070426
835507LV00021B/2829
* 9 7 8 0 9 8 9 5 8 5 0 0 2 *